NEW PLAINS REVIEW

I0553512

SPRING 2014

Editors and Staff

Executive Editor	Shay Rahm
Production Chief	Michelle Waggoner
Editors-in-Chief	Christina Morel
	Kaylee Kain
Managing Editor	Maggie McGee
Poetry Editor	Haley Rapacz
Assistant Poetry Editors	Phillip Harvey
	Marianna Bennett
	William Godwin
Fiction Editor	Cherie Poertner
Assistant Fiction Editors	Caitlin Bell
	Michael Bemus
	Brendon Yuill
Nonfiction Editor	Maggie McGee
Assistant Nonfiction Editors	Meagan Hover
	Rachel Brocklehurst
Social Media	Rachel Brocklehurst
	William Godwin
Webmaster	William Andrews

New Plains Review Publishing Group
University of Central Oklahoma
Edmond, Oklahoma

NEW PLAINS REVIEW

ISBN-10: 0983735751
ISBN-13: 978-0-9837357-5-5

New Plains Review is a literary journal published each academic semester, sponsored by the English Department, College of Liberal Arts, at the University of Central Oklahoma. The image found on every cover of *New Plains Review* issue since 2000 is based on a painting titled "Phantom Warriors" by acclaimed Native American artist and UCO alumnus Sherman Chaddlesone.

New Plains Review
English Department, Box 184
University of Central Oklahoma
100 North University Drive
Edmond, Oklahoma 73034
(405) 974-5613

newplainsreview@gmail.com
www.libarts.uco.edu/english/newplains

Submission Information: *New Plains Review* accepts original work in prose, poetry, drama, fiction, art, and photography. Submissions are accepted by email. For editorial guidelines, please visit the website.

Ordering Information: Pricing for subscriptions, current and back issues are available through the website.

Equal Opportunity Statement: In compliance with Title VI and Title VII of the Civil Rights Act of 1964, Executive Order 11246 as amended, Title IX of The Education Amendments of 1972, Sections 503 and 504 of The Rehabilitation Act of 1973, the Americans With Disabilities Act of 1990, the Family and Medical Leave Act of 1993, the Civil Rights Acwt of 1991, and other Federal Laws and Regulations, the University of Central Oklahoma does not discriminate on the basis of race, color, national origin, sex, age, religion, handicap, disability, or status as a veteran in any of its policies, practices or procedures; this includes but is not limited to admissions, employment, financial aid, and educational services.

Foreword

"But however naive I might be, I do feel that books have a unique way of stopping time in a particular moment and saying: "Let's not forget this."
– Dave Eggers

This Spring publication of the *New Plains Review* has been a combined effort of diverse talents by each of our hardworking student editors. This issue integrates authors with various perspectives and voices from our culture today. We have chosen distinctive entries for our Poetry, Nonfiction, and Fiction sections which highlight topics such as the natural state of life, the emotion of rebellion, and the controversial subject of infidelity. A wonderful aspect of writing is the way in which it allows anyone to voice their unique experiences — no matter how difficult, comedic, heartwarming, or abstract they might be. A perfect example of this colorful abstraction is our selected artwork by Dr. Ernest Williamson III. We keep our writers and audience in mind as we select our stories and edit them. We hope to embolden our readers to write and create, whether it be a short poem about a moment in their lives, a tale with compelling images and creations that don't exist, or creating art that can change our perspective. As dedicated editors with a love for publishing art and the written word, we are confident both our hard work and the authors' multifarious works we have selected are aptly displayed herein.

We present the Spring 2014 issue of *New Plains Review.*
Christina Morel and Kaylee Kain
Co-Editors-in-Chief

Contents

Poetry

Sarah Montgomery
Listening for Birds in Spring

> *"Picture windows which often used to frame a scene splashed with the red of forty or fifty cardinals and crowded with other species, seldom permitted a view of as many as a bird or two at a time."*
> – Rachel Carson, *Silent Spring*

Sitting on the porch, my feet are full of rivers,
blue veins coursing so fast I almost hear them.
Across the street is a grey metal barn and the sound
of boys bouncing rocks off the tin roof. A creaking
railroad track bisects the town, a rush of faces
in the windows whenever the train roars by.

I hear the sound of a worn pickup puttering,
sharp backfire, the painful ease and release
of yellow bus breaks at the corner, the neighbor's t.v.
and a static humming radio from a garage somewhere.
A phone rings shrilly and a lawnmower growls.
A plane buzzes, dipping low below to spray fields.

It's hard to hear the faint chortle of a sparrow,
the sharp chirp of robin, birds numbering two,
no more than three, whistling through the noise.

George Freek

A Poem About Birdwatching (After TU FU)

In the trees starlings chatter.
Their behavior is noisy
and erratic. Among birds,
they're nasty fanatics.
Over their heads, the moon
falls like a feather
into a frozen bed.
But they pay it no heed.
They're like we are,
concerned with transitory needs.
And are their thoughts
also full of mindless chatter?
And like young lovers,
do they make poems,
which pretend to glean
meanings from
such unpromising matter?

Michael Catherwood

For Silence

There are no choirs to accompany us
and morning begins as you turn to the window
where the backyard recedes without sorrow.
In the sterile haze a red-tailed hawk cuts

the air, plays against the roar of distant cars.
Where does it all come together
and do our plans hold up to promise? Stare
ahead into the evening moon and the far-

off years retreat like dirt roads or quasars.
Of course there are the seams left in our hearts
but love has become easier and silent.

There is the tree and the brave unfettered
sun. There is the curled song of the skylark.
Wind begins in silence and builds in the distance.

Iain Macdonald

Bayonets and
Carpet Slippers

The young men returned, carrying
with them their night-sweat hells
of Japanese officers beheading
their best friend in some steaming jungle,
or fellow sailors screaming their
too-slow last in an ocean of oil and fire
after the German wolf pack struck;
and they went back to their jobs in the
shipyards and mines, back to their
Friday night pint and Saturday football
pools, back to their mothers' home baking
and their wives' impeccable housekeeping.

And if some of them drowned themselves
in the bottle, or wandered late-night
onto the rail line as the London to Glasgow
express thundered down, well, "He was
a good man, but troubled," and all his friends
and neighbors showed up for the funeral,
standing bare-headed in the rain, before
going back to their daily toil and racing
pigeons and garden allotments and a summer
week by the seaside, keeping their silence,
because that is what you did.

And so the fifties became the sixties, and
then the seventies, in a country increasingly
difficult to understand, and they became
outdated, redundant, even vaguely ridiculous,
to their own children most of all.

And now it is another world, and we, their
middle-aged offspring, lower their caskets
into the wet soil, and part of why we weep
is because it is too late to cry, "No, come back!
I want to know. Please, pull up a chair, pour
another cup of tea. Please. Won't you tell us
                    what you saw? Tell us how it was."

Daryl Muranaka

Canyons

Mom once called Mt. Waialeale
the wettest spot on Earth, where no one
goes, where you wouldn't want to,
where the rain is measured in feet

and the water falls
down all the yards of the all the miles,
dodging, cutting the earth, at first shallow,
then deeper and deeper

through the strata of the island's body.
A sharp wound splayed out, open
to the naked air. The more interesting layers
exposed. The green stretching towards the sun.

And I wonder aren't we like that —
our crust, hard yet green. Our passions
open to be carved up by time
and exposed to an unforgiving light.

When I was old enough to know
what would help and young enough
to know what would hurt,
I let each moment rest on me

each new chance to feel, to know add up.
I added new skin over the old
until I was ready, new earth
waiting to be explored.

And then there was you, the idea of you,
the touch of you and your idea of me,
the obstacle of me. Did your love flow
like water, cutting me?

Did you cover me like a heavy, looming cloud?
Or did I choose you as the earth embraces
the ever constant rain and let your love flow
in steadfast rivers and disappear into the sea?

Daniel Ames

The Stoned Volunteers

the volunteers are stoned
the hashish and absinthe slowly departed
revealing the cold, gray battlefield
smoke breathing its way across the depressed valleys

they turned and looked behind them
a river black and bottomless
filled with the mysterious rhythm of the South

ahead they saw the fury
the jagged crystalline teeth
as a figure in white retreated

they realized surrender was out of the question
face forward, dawn's mist clinging to their stubble
they smiled and loaded their rifles

their breath hung in the air like morphine fumes
cooked in cast iron over a prostitute's campfire
the charge was glorious
and brief

Joseph Dorazio
The Vulture

A bare-headed sort above ground,
nearer the clouds, he gracefully
soars in circles. On landing
he's a different bird:
the stork's doppelganger,
an awkward sideways hop,
wings raised as pyramids on either side,
hideously bald and lappet-faced,
red wattle, dips his head in and out
like a pen in an inkwell.
The mortician of Memphis,
he's content to leave the eyes to crows,
tail to a jackal. He peels from the anus,
bearded disemboweler,
gorges on putrefied innards until
his crop is carrion-stuffed.
Praise Nekhbet. Praise
Pharaoh, whose rarified liver
was never gobbled like this.

Robert Karaszi

The Art of Chrysanthemums

We swing like silk or snow
   swept over mesa flats.

Though in the pith of fall,
   leaves twitch red
through the eddy, at eventide.

We sit long-sleeved in a river house
   mull over music,
that warms
   ice creatures.

Today I raked a melody
   with syllables culled from your lips.
But I miss you when you gather

   chrysanthemums each morning;
and on return,
   float their painted tongues
in glass bowls.

Chrysanthemums round patio light
   remind me of our first autumn,
when you held my glove
   in the Venus noon.

Darling. This garden is art, verged on the obsessive
   but I heed the artistry in your labors,
I hold them dear, their desires unafraid to conjure wings
   that they may conjure flight.

Upon twisting your wrist, caught
   in the spindrift of creation,
you could no longer heave soil to stack.

I tended fresh earth in delicious seclusion,
   and laced your pond with chrysanthemum gold.

So come! Meet me under ribboned white
   where autumn hovers, and the sun sidles near —
as the murmurs of our harmonies hold.

William Miller

Picture of Me and My Son

He's 10. I'm 40.

We sit at a folding table
piled with copies
of a mystery novel

I wrote and sold
around the state.
He traveled with me.

He's a quiet, curious kid,
only asks questions
about serious things —
his dead bird,
a flood in China ...

After a week, we go
home to a rented
row house in a poor,
beautiful neighborhood.

People sit on stoops,
know each other's names,
watch out for the kids.

And my son grows up
in the empty spaces
between parents
who fight
for and against
a neat lawn, little crime,
all-white schools ...

Now, he's been to rehab
for rum, Ecstacy,
lives in a halfway house
in California.

Alone, I take lithium
live on a government check;
my book is out of print.

But we talk on cell phones
for hours: movies,
drugs, the war
he'd never fight
even if there was a draft.

He doesn't have any
regrets — it took every hit,
every drink to get
him there.

Once, we talked
about Christ, how
on the cross he was
tempted by Satan to live
a safe, normal life:

a wife and children,
old age, an easy death.

But he found his voice,
shouted who he was,
claimed his wounds
at the end.

Michael Catherwood
Modern Scenes

Topography floats on the lake
and collapses. We no longer
exist; water rings sink
into each other, the watery

glass a still life of gray
soft concrete. Lines in grocery
stores are spirals of redundancy —
unrecognizable music trickles

from the turrets of cereal. We are
pale and seduced and ghostly
with our essentials bagged up
neat as suns. We need

this emptiness, this formidable
distraction. White noise
fills the universe, spins in
parking lots; stars flutter

like birds; jugglers dance
in our childhoods, the only color
now. Humor might
find us, strike us

down when the dull
blades of our minds break
apart, when long evenings
carry away our indiferent tortures.

Fiction

Todd Easton Mills

A Deer-Colored Arroyo

Douglas, who had been a child actor, lived in the gardener's house at the Clark Estate in Montecito. The main house was gated with twelve thousand square feet, two tennis courts, a pool with a 50's style diving board, and a freestanding six-car garage. The best view of the ocean was from the Wisteria covered pergola overlooking the rose garden, and although Douglas had been invited to "swim whenever he liked," he was content to spend his afternoons on the patio of his tiny stone house or take a walk along the stream where Chumash once hunted deer.

Penelope, his mother, gym-fit and blonde, brushed the leaves from a peeling, wrought-iron table to lay down her cell phone.

"Would you like soap and water and a sponge, Mother?"

"You could ask the gardener to blow the leaves," Penelope said.

"I could, I guess. But I like it rustic."

"That's what you call it. Do people visit you back here?"

"No friends, fans, or hangers-on."

"I hope you aren't referring to your business manager."

"No, Mother. You were the best business manager a boy could have. I just want to try it stripped down for awhile."

"You say that, but you are the guest of people who live in a twenty-five million dollar house." There was a mechanical chirp. Penelope scrolled her iPhone and looked up. "Why do you turn off your phone? I can never reach you."

"I'm practicing silence."

"You're not talking?" she asked, surprised.

"Just a day now and then."

"That's funny."

"It's not my idea. Larry Hagman did it all the time."

"To sober up," she said flatly.

He pushed back a flap of tawny locks, exposing a bald patch.

"Douglas, if you don't work, the world is going to forget about you."

"That's fine. I'm too old to be a child actor."

"You mean a star?"

Douglas sighed. "I guess."

Antonio, the Mexican gardener, finished the lawn with a hand mower. He asked if they wanted him to blow the patio.

"No, Antonio, it's fine," Douglas said. "Mother, did you park in the driveway or on the street?"

"In the driveway, of course," Penelope said.

"That's not good. I'm not allowed to use the driveway."

"Not allowed?"

Penelope walked around the patio with her hands on her hips. She picked up a book on the garden table next to Douglas's reading chair.

"You gave me that book when I was fourteen," Douglas said.

"I don't remember."

"It's *Walden*," Douglas said reverently.

August 5: I have been exploring the seasonal creek that winds around the property on the northwest side. It goes down the hill through a tunnel of vines into the Pacific Ocean. There are old oaks and sycamores with vines strangling the trees like wrestlers. The water is slow, clear for three or four inches. Worms push up in the morning, and tiny fish flicker in the pools. I haven't uttered a word in ten days. I wonder if I will have a strong or weak voice when I talk again. I want to try it for a month.

August 6: I saw a deer today, a doe I think. She is an astonishing jumper. I can't estimate her weight. I would look it up on my iPhone except I have promised myself no more Google, Internet, or television.

August 9: As an actor, I was an instrument for reproducing emotion. Now I reproduce silence. I sit on the rocks and watch the stream go by. Sometimes I imagine Chumash sitting beside me; bare-breasted women with woven armbands. They stripe their faces with clay from the stream, while children hunt birds with featherless arrows.

August 10: Water is beautiful, depending on the sunlight and the bottom. I've owned pools with white and gray bottoms. White bottoms make brilliant diamonds that expand like steel gates when you dive in. Gray bottoms stain easily and reflect nothing.

August 15: I was famous and I loved it. I was the million-to-one shot. Who doesn't want to be rich and famous? I loved it for twenty years, then I hated it. It had nothing to do with the media. I liked high-speed chases with paparazzi hanging out the window to get the shot. When you are a child, you are supposed to be the center of attention. I could channel fear and sadness. I could cry on command. I was a well-tuned instrument of love and hate.

August 26: Today I watched a red-headed woodpecker drill the oak that hangs over my patio. There are other birds in the forest as loud as the woodpecker — like the crows — but none so cruel. They've pecked my oak until it looks like Swiss cheese.

With the Clarks away in New York, Penelope felt she could pop in on Douglas. She brought fresh bread and cheese, sometimes kipper snacks and vegetable soup from Pierre LaFond. There was a dense fog in Ventura and clouds in Santa Barbara, but in Montecito, in the Golden Triangle, it was sunny and warm.

"What do you do all day, Douglas?"

"Less and less."

"Are you writing?"

"A little, in my journal."

"Why don't you write a script?"

"Maybe someday. I'm happy in my garden."

"It's not your garden. It belongs to a very successful hedge fund manager," Penelope laughed.

"I'm not wearing shoes. It's how I stay grounded."

"Do you say these things to irritate me?"

"Uh-huh."

"You're funny. Why don't you write comedy?"

Douglas had disabled his phone by reversing the battery. His mother was his only visitor. He didn't mind that she brought lunch. He spent too much time preparing food and cleaning up. He read *Walden* and sometimes he would recite passages from memory:

"How many immortal souls have I met, crushed and smothered under their load ... their misfortune was they inherited farms, houses, barns, cattle, farming tools. Better be born in an open pasture and suckled by a wolf."

"Your lips are moving, Douglas. Are you saying your prayers?" Penelope joked.

"The better part of man is soon plunged into the soil for compost," he said in a forceful voice.

"You're scaring me. I brought snacks. Shall I make coffee?"

November 15: There was a gusher today when one of the sprinkler heads blew off, sending water up twenty feet. Antonio arrived an hour later and needed to turn off the water at the main valve to fix it. While I waited, I made coffee with stream water.

November 16: What are the necessities of life? Food, clothing, fuel? Heating fuel, maybe, in Concord, but not Montecito. What would Thoreau think about my winterless paradise?

November 27: I shave in the creek, but not in the same place every day. I like to find a deep pool. The morning stillness has made me an invisible man. I am so much a part of it, I can walk on sharp leaves and bits of pine cone without shoes. If I were thrown into the lion's den like Daniel, the lion would look through me. I am just another rock. With my shirt off I am four rocks: my stomach is a boulder; my chest, two skipping stones; my head a piece of granite.

November 18: Today I tracked a deer along the muddy bank. After a few hundred feet, its footprints vanished and the pricks of a leaping mouse appeared.

The roof of the mansion was hidden by fog. Penelope knocked on the window with her heavy, gold ring. Douglas was naked under the sheet but got out of bed with no modesty. Throughout his childhood and teenage years, this was the routine, because it was Penelope's job to wake him for early calls.

"Open the door, Douglas. Why is it locked?"

"God, Mother. What time is it?"

"I have something important to tell you."

"Can you come back later?"

"No, it's really important."

Penelope sat on a chair in the middle of the room, her left leg twitching, a tick he hadn't seen before.

"I'm afraid I have some bad news. You better sit down."

"Bad news? Your health, Mother?" Douglas looked at her closely.

"There is a problem with your trust account. I called our accountant and his phone is disconnected. I got worried and checked with our broker. He said the accountant has been trading in the account and it's gone badly. He bought Canadian mining stock and a leveraged ETF fund that went against him. There isn't much left."

"How much?"

"If you cashed in today, you would be down ninety-five percent. You need to go back to work."

Douglas opened the door for his mother.

"Don't blame me. I didn't steal the money."

December 5: The woodpeckers peck incessantly. There are fifty oaks on the property, but they have concentrated their torture on my patio tree. Why this one? A little pecking would feel like a back scratch. But this poor old man suffers death by a thousand cuts.

December 7: I am taking longer walks. Today I climbed to the top of the hill which required breaking large branches. The view of Santa Cruz island is hidden by the limbs of oaks. To get a better view, I climbed a tree. Afterward I jumped down into soft dirt and found footprints of a mountain lion. I am sure it was a mountain lion and not a bobcat. If I see it, I will snap my fingers or click rocks. They are shy and no threat because they have plenty of deer to eat.

December 11: This morning a woodpecker woke me by pecking the drainpipe, and it sounded like a jackhammer. I told Mother I don't want to see her. She said she wouldn't come back unless she had an audition for me. I'm not going to reconnect my phone. I can last for a year with the money that's left.

December 19: The Clarks aren't coming home this Christmas. I have the place to myself. The pool is heated, so I started swimming. It feels good to do laps and flips off the board. After my swim I wash the chlorine out of my eyes in the creek. I am the Transcendentalist who likes the pool. Is this a betrayal of nature? What would Thoreau say?

⟍

"You look tan," Penelope said.
Douglas nodded.
"And you lost weight."
"I'm trying."
"That's not a good thing."
"Not good?"
"I had a conversation with a casting director. They are remaking Deliverance — they want you for the Ned Beatty part."

⟍

"My excuse for not lecturing against the use of tobacco is that I never chewed it ... I dreamed that I might gather wild herbs to sell to the villagers, but trade curses everything it handles. I prefer some things to others, and especially value my freedom. I do not want to spend my time earning money to buy rich carpets or fine furniture."

⟍

December 21: My feet are getting tougher. I can leap from rock to rock and am more flexible. I haven't weighed myself, but I can't see my toes. Today I shaved in a pool with little fish and they didn't swim away. My beard is yellow, but it grows fast. Shaving is my only regular habit.

⟍

On December 26th, three news helicopters hovered above the swimming pool of the Clark Estate, one so low it rimmed the water with concentric circles. Competing networks got shots of the main house and tennis courts, but the arroyo was too overgrown to see the creek. An aging anchorman, boosted by the gardener's ladder, climbed the wall and reported from the pergola with the springboard framed in the background.

Henry Johnson, the youngest deputy, found the body with the spine bitten through and half the head missing. He asked the sheriff if he had ever seen a mountain lion attack. He hadn't. "I thought they gave humans a wide berth."

"I don't know," said Calvin Green, "maybe it was an older lion, or a young one learning to hunt. I know if you see one, you shout. You raise your hands to look as big as you can, but you stay calm. If you have a stick, you fight back. A rock is better than a stick because a stick can snap." His hand grazed his leather holster. "You didn't move the body, did you?"

"No, the lion dragged it here," Johnson said.

The body was partially covered by a clump of poison oak.

"The head is really bad," Green said. "You just hope he was dead before it started feeding on the shoulders and stomach."

*

December 24: "Nothing is so impoverishing as wealth." I am getting to the essence of it. "Should I go to heaven or go fishing?" I've made up my mind — I won't take the Ned Beatty role. I won't be the fat man tied to a tree and raped by hillbillies. This is the right decision. I know because I have never felt so calm and at one with the world. Silence makes the voice weaker then stronger. I'm going down to the river to shave. It's quiet today — no singing birds or woodpeckers drumming. Maybe I'll go back up the hill to collect firewood.

Doug Sanders

If You Could Ask God One Thing, What Would It Be?

Just after my divorce had been processed completely, I found myself cleaning out the basement of the home I had been paying into for the past 20 years (and was now being kicked out of) when I came across this old shoebox that was filled with a bunch of stuff from college. By all measurements, I was having a terrible year. That winter, my 16-year-old son had died in a car crash the week after he got his driver's license. Rather than cause my wife and I to bond closer together, the whole thing tore us apart rather brutally. The three of us used to have Thursday Game Night and play a new board game every week like one of those happy families you see on television commercial breaks. But after he died, the only game we played anymore was one we created when we were drunk after painfully quiet and awkward dinners. The new game was called:

Who's To Blame More For Greg's Death?

As far as I know, nobody has sold the idea yet to Hasbro or Parker Brothers.

We would always play this new game of ours right after a few too many glasses of wine (not the fun too many glasses we used to share that would result in wild sex on our back porch, but the I-want-to-forget-that-I-actually-exist kind).

We'd become so pissed off about the shitty lives we had seemed to wake up in on the day Officer Daniels knocked on our front door and described how Greg's Jeep SUV rolled off Maple Road — the same road that I had driven him on a thousand times before for daycare, soccer practice and other things I can't even talk about anymore in public without breaking down.

So I was there in the basement of the house that I no longer could call home, feeling terribly nostalgic for the memories of my college years, the days when my biggest worry was where to find free beer and how to not fail out of my Economics course. I crumbled down right down on the floor and put that old shoebox on my lap.

That old beat-up cardboard shoebox looked like a real, genuine, working time machine.

I opened it cautiously. Examining every scrap with careful concentration. There were countless ticket stubs to concerts I only semi-remembered and photographs of people I didn't remember at all. I felt like an archaeologist digging up relics from an era that the entire human race, most surprisingly of all me, had forgotten about completely.

I had felt so isolated and distant from the people in my current life, my son was gone to … well, somewhere unknown … and my wife thought I was the biggest piece of shit she had ever come across. The whole time in the lawyer's office, the tone in her voice as she described our marriage sounded like she was describing in spectacular detail the most disgusting gas station restroom in the whole United States.

Yes, I had a few well-intentioned friends who tried to sympathize with my situation over after-work drinks, but as I would be eagerly flagging down the bartender for my third gin on the rocks, they'd be politely saying no to their second light beer, they were fine thanks, explaining how they needed to drive home, back to the families and homes they still had, and at those moments, it always became obvious that none of them actually understood the mess my life had become in a few short months.

So when I opened that shoebox, I thought I would be able to reconnect with someone who might understand what I was going through: the old me from college. Surely, of all people, he would understand.

But with each photograph or old memento I didn't remember clearly, I felt more and more isolated from even him. The person I used to be. He was almost unrecognizable. I felt the incredible urge to scream at him. There in the dingy basement among my wife's gaudy Christmas decorations and my half-finished DIY projects, I wanted to yell at the top of my lungs to that 20-year-old me. I wanted to scream until my vocal chords started bleeding:

"Heads up you fucking moron! The shit is about to really hit the fan."

But I didn't. I somehow knew my voice wouldn't carry across two decades. Even if it did, that guy in the photographs probably wouldn't have listened. He was too drunk and too stupid. And what I hated about him the most was how he was too happy. Too happy to care.

That asshole was so damn happy.

Instead of yelling, I decided to continue looking through the entire box before I would throw it in the garbage for good and say goodbye to another person I used to know dearly.

That's when I stumbled upon a big manila envelope marked in big black permanent marker letters: *The Cosmic Complaint Box.* I opened it up and there was a special project — if you could even call it a project — that came from a long night of drinking between my sophomore roommate and I.

And I recalled the night we came up with the idea with surprising clarity, at least most of it, like it had just happened the night before. We had gotten good and drunk on a few cases of cheap beer after just returning back to campus from winter break. We started out sharing tales of our awkward adventures back home. He had an older brother who had just returned from boot camp and was now teaching him the proper etiquette at strip clubs near their hometown. I had an ex-girlfriend who bored me to death when we were dating, but for some reason she now had me interested in her — at least, interested enough to take her out to dinner occasionally and make out with from time to time. We drank more. Shared more awkward tales. Kept drinking until we were drunk and carefree enough to share our biggest complaints.

Then, I don't know where it came from exactly, but I looked at him and asked him plainly, like I was asking the time of day, "If you could ask God one thing, what would it be?"

He told me his answer and asked me and I told him mine. And as serious as blood brothers taking the oath, we promised not to tell anyone else. So I won't tell you what either of us said.

The beer never seemed to end and after an hour or so we started wondering how the rest of the world would answer the same question. We reasoned that the answer might explain why the world around us was so fucked up. And before you knew it, we were breaking into the undergraduate newspaper office where he worked to use the industrial printing machine to print out about 200 or 300 copies of the survey we had created, each on a single sheet of paper and with only one question at the top of the otherwise blank pages:

If you could ask God one thing, what would it be?

From there, we were convinced this was the best idea anyone had ever come with in the history of mankind. We started looking up random addresses on the internet, sealing and putting stamps on stacks of envelopes after filling them with the survey and a bunch of other empty smaller envelopes that had prepaid postage and our real apartment address.

Anyways, we returned from the mailbox and that's when my roommate pulled out a bottle of whiskey his dad had gotten him for Christmas. Before he opened it, he stood up on the kitchen chair like a dignified politician, declared that he had fully intended to save this bottle for a special occasion and then added this direct quote:

"But fuck it."

We passed out as the sun was coming up. After we woke up, after we sobered up, we laughed about our survey. We talked about how ridiculous the whole idea had been and how no one would ever waste their time filling out such an absurd thing. Classes started back up the next day and we got into the swing of normal college life again.

Then, a few weeks later, we started to receive mysterious envelopes in the mail. We opened them and found answers to the question we didn't think anyone would bother answering. Lo and behold, people from as far as Alaska and Maine had answered our little drunken survey.

In the basement, I sat with my back against the wall and began reading those old replies to our one-question survey. Here are some of those answers, in no particular order:

"Were you a baby once, like, you know, a little God baby?"

"Are there aliens?"

"Where did my brother go after he hung himself? I've heard you're not really too keen on the suicide thing but he is, I mean, was, he was such a good kid. Like there was this one time when we were little and Ms. Scruffs, our dog, got sick and you could just tell how much pain she was in by the way she wouldn't even bark like she always used to. She wouldn't even eat her favorite food that she always used to devour. So then my brother, he was only 6 at the time, but no matter how much Mom and Dad tried to stop him, my brother would sit next to our Ms. Scruffs all night — he did it for three nights in a row — just petting her, giving her water and all that until Ms. Scruffs finally died."

"What do you do for fun?"

"Why did you make all the food that's bad for you taste so damn good? I mean why not just make every vegetable taste like a big juicy bacon cheeseburger? Why not make sugar taste like mud or sand? That way, almost everyone would be healthier. Right now, you've made cholesterol-inducing deep fried chicken taste absolutely delicious and celery taste like cardboard and that just seems so unnecessarily cruel. That's more than one question, isn't it?"

"What's the deal with time?"

"Why don't I believe in you?"

"I wouldn't ask anything. I would give God a piece of my mind though. I would just stand right there and say: You ought to be ashamed of yourself. We are really suffering down here. I have been working seven days a week for the last 2 years without a single day off and you take a break after 6 days. You shouldn't have taken that seventh day off. Look around, there's so much you forgot to finish."

"When my wife and I have sex, are you seeing that? I know you're supposed to be able to see everything. So does that mean you are watching us do the deed? To be honest, I think we'd both be kind of into that."

"Where were you when I needed you? I waited and waited and waited but you never came around."

"Can you help us all get along down here? For God's sake, or, I guess for your sake, we're literally fighting over you, claiming that we know what you really want when none of us actually know that for a fact, and we're blowing each other and the planet to bits in the process."

"Are we alone?"

"Abraham seems like he had a screw loose. Tell the truth, were you even involved in that whole almost-sacrifice-your-son-to-prove-your-faith charade?"

"Where do we go?"

"I'm not even going to ask you anymore to make him understand my lifestyle or what it means for me (his only daughter) to be a lesbian. We're way past all that. But will you please, please, please stop my father from getting so blindingly drunk during those awkward holiday dinners and repeatedly asking my girlfriend and me in front of the whole family: *"So which one of you is the boy?"*

"Will I die alone?"

"Do you have sexual genitalia? If so, is it male, female or … both?"

"What's outside the universe?"

"Is there a purpose to all this? This doesn't make any sense. They tell me if I pay close attention, I'll start to understand but no matter how much attention I pay, I don't understand. It just gets more and more confusing."

And after reading all of these surveys twice, I sat there completely still with the shoebox on my lap, overwhelmed by all the confusion and pain life becomes, before an inescapable urge came over me to frantically search the entire house for a permanent marker that I would eventually find in the junk drawer of the kitchen. There, on the counter, next to the toaster, I flattened out one of those old surveys and scratched out the stranger's handwritten answer. Below the question, in big bold letters, I wrote down the thought that had been haunting me for months, the feeling I had secretly been carrying around since the minute Officer Daniels told us in the front hallway about how my son would not be returning home that evening.

Why didn't you take me? It should have been me.

Phyllis Green

Jesus Doesn't Like Bubblegum

Vange Klosters, the healer, was a whisper of a woman, about size four with a husky, whiskey voice that boomed without the need of a microphone. She had earned her fluffy, white hair by the age of thirty-eight and it fell to the middle of her back like a horse's mane. Her eyes were brown and beady (sparrow eyes) and her lips were painted a deep fuchsia. On stage she always wore a white robe so everyone would think of her as an angel, but on the bus she wore a pink tank top, red short shorts, and strappy high heels.

I began to work for Vange when I was seven. She relieved orphanages of some of their kids and I was one. She pretended we were adopted, but truly we weren't. Still, she took pretty good care of us. I was healed of my crippledness at every service. I had to wear iron braces that cut into my legs and left blood marks that never went away. I was "saved" all over the country in barns, at county fairs, in town halls, in stranger's homes, and along the roadsides. Our bus would pull into town and word and our flyers would get out, often by gossip, and crowds would gather and want to be healed from their various illnesses and disfigurements, even ugliness or big noses, but mostly it was cancer they wanted to be delivered from. Vange would preach and holler and say, "DO YOU BELIEVE?" and "JESUS WANTS YOU TO STOP BEING ASSHOLES AND BIG FAT SINNERS," and things like that, and that's why people loved her. And then those of us from the bus — me and the others — would give up our sins. One of the kids would cry, another kid vomit, then I would miraculously walk and everyone would praise Jesus that we were healed.

Some of the townspeople seem to be healed too, but I'm not sure if it actually took. You see, I'm sure you do, that I was never a cripple. I just played one.

I usually sat on the bus with the boy who was a leper. Frank was his name. He wasn't a leper, but I actually wondered by the time I was nine if he could speak because he hadn't said one word in two years.

We got paid five dollars each service unless Vange didn't get enough in the collection plate to cover gas and food for us and enough for her to add to her bank account and buy stuff. She was especially fond of rings and she had some beauties. She let us girls try them on sometimes. I about died and went to heaven when I tried on the aquamarine. She also had a suitcase full of fancy, lacy bras and panties which we envied. Vange tried to teach us to use our pay smartly. She didn't want us to buy comics or too much candy. She regularly informed us that "JESUS DOESN'T LIKE BUBBLEGUM," so I mostly spent my money on candy corn, a movie magazine, and orange nail polish.

It turned out Frank, my bus mate, was a mute. Vange couldn't cure his throat, only his tattooed leprosy. But Frank was active in other ways, and when we were both fifteen I ended up with an alien in my belly. That's what Vange called it and she healed my belly with a coat hanger.

Then she had to do it again when I was sixteen. After that, Vange fired Frank and there wasn't anything he could say to defend himself because 1. He was a mute who couldn't say a dang word and 2. He had put the alien there. Frank just took his $75 in savings and started walking the opposite way the bus was headed and I never saw him again. I just hoped he would find another healer because his leprosy scars looked so authentic. Like, who wouldn't believe he had it?

Vange liked to brag that she had healed more folks than Aimee Semple McPherson and Kathryn Kuhlman combined. She said she was following in their faith healing footsteps but she did it her way and not their fussy-fussy goody two-shoes way.

Our bus drivers changed rather often. Vange would look out into the crowds and whisper, "There's a hunk." Pretty soon she'd be chatting him up and then we'd have a new bus driver. Then the new hunk would wink and flirt with Vange, which made her giggle, and soon she'd be treating us all to ice cream cones and saying, "Now disappear for a while like little darlings." I tell you, that bus would rock like crazy.

There came a time when I felt so low and couldn't eat; something was wrong, I just knew it. And Vange got all worried and against all her rules, took me to an emergency room and they poked and x-rayed and took vials of blood and my vitals and all that and finally told Vange her daughter had it. The horrid stuff. The worst. That stuff everyone wanted to be rid of. And I, Justine, only nineteen, had it bad.

Vange fell into a valley of depression. That's what she called it and I knew it was true 'cause she got rid of the Italian hunk, Mario, and hired Estelle, an ugly woman with no taste in clothes, to drive our bus.

She said she could not cure me. I begged her. I said, "Ask me if I believe! Ask me to confess my sins! Tell Jesus I may be a god-damned liar, but I love him. Tell Jesus to shape it up and take this crap out of me. Tell him, Vange. You can do it!"

Finally when she must have feared I was about to go, she perked up and ordered everyone out of the bus and into a field of fresh mown hay.

"SHOUT IT OUT YOU SINNERS," she hollered. "LET ME HEAR YOU PRAY TO JESUS TO SAVE OUR LITTLE SISTER. I DON'T HEAR YOU! LOUDER! ARE YOU ASKING JESUS TO SAVE HER OR ARE YOU TWIDDLING YOUR

THUMBS? PRAY YOUR LITTLE ASSES OFF! THIS IS JUSTINE WE'RE
TALKING ABOUT!"

And then she addressed me. I was being held up by Estelle and Nell. Nell
was our brain tumor. But when they lifted their arms up to implore Jesus, I
sighed and floated to the new mown hay and lay there like a deflated balloon.

"GET UP SINNER AND CONFESS YOUR SINS! JUSTINE, DO YOU BELIEVE?
SAY IT!"

"I believe. I believe, Vange. I believe with all my heart."

And I did believe at that moment. And I felt covered in light. In the haze
I saw them all trooping onto the bus and then the bus driving away.

I lay there watching a tiny black field mouse running between the sticks
of left over hay. And I believed and believed like you wouldn't believe.

Jennifer Boddicker

The Ultimate Cliché

Chad the waiter loomed over our table, shooting impatient breaths from his gold-studded nose. My husband didn't seem to notice, absorbed as he was in the menu. The top of David's head was visible as he scanned the entrees, and I glimpsed, for the very first time, his shiny pink scalp peeking through. David's hair was thick in front, barely receding at all, but here was this thin spot at his crown. It reminded me of the lab mice I once euthanized in the name of science, skin evident through mottled fur as they twitched and gasped their last.

Hats, I thought.

I'd never been a fan, but hats were made for this, to protect, to cover up the scalp. Maybe I'd get one for David's birthday, a nice Indiana Jones type.

David deserved a sexy hat.

Of course, he wouldn't wear it in a restaurant, and there would still be that thin spot to contend with. I'd have to get used to it. Not think of dead mice. David deserved better than that. And no doubt, there were things about me David would rather not see. Crow's feet gathered in skin that was previously smooth; a pooched-out stomach that was flat before the birth of two children. A number of declining features he must have noticed and looked away from.

The restaurant I'd chosen for his birthday was full of couples, young and old, straight and gay, awash in conversation and clinking cutlery. Food Attaché it was called, and it was all the rage. The décor was minimal, the aromas delectable: lemon and basil, bread and smoked fish, a braid of scent woven among dark tables and chairs. White washed walls were hung with cunning modern artwork, which evoked vegetables or genitals, depending upon your perspective. Since I was both hungry and horny, I could see it either way.

"Nice cucumber," I said, pointing to the painting above our table.

Though I had ordered already, linguine in clam sauce, it was only then that Chad the waiter seemed to notice I was there. He sported a look of sudden recognition. *Ah,* it said. *This person has a vagina.*

"Nice if you like cucumbers," he replied. "Personally, I prefer that one."

He pointed to the wall beyond my husband's head. It featured a painting of an avocado, split in two, with curved black edges open to lush flesh that was pitted to reveal a shadowed and mysterious cleft. The rawness of the painting made me shiver unexpectedly, a series of small quakes along my inner thighs.

"It's lovely," I said.

"Beautiful," he agreed, looking right at me.

He's flirting, I realized, with mild shock. The waiter was flirting with me, and my husband sat two feet away. It was gratifying, but I quickly broke eye contact and stared into the depths of my fizzy white wine. Maybe he knew, I thought, with a tiny flame of mortification. Maybe he sensed it. Was it so obvious, the lack of conjugal bliss?

Regardless, I wasn't so far gone that I needed to flirt with waiters, especially not Chad, who cultivated a moody look and probably fancied himself a writer, like every third person in town. Chad wore all black, black glasses frames, and an unsavory square of matching black hair perched precisely between his lips and chin. A soul patch, I'd heard it called, as though facial fuzz signified depth of character.

Likewise, a scruff of beard darkened David's jaw. I tried not to let my irritation show as we left the house that evening. David knew I didn't like facial hair. I didn't like the way it scraped my face when we kissed. It had been awhile, but back in the days when we made love with the rising sun, his morning stubble left marks which I found unseemly, mainly because I taught biology at the local community college, and suspected that certain young men in my class entertained lascivious notions about me as I paced the front of the lecture hall. Not that I was gorgeous. I was an average looking thirty-five year old woman, a bit tall and lanky for conventional tastes. However, for the male students in my class, every woman, save their own mother, was a possible conquest. I found their roving gaze flattering, but with each new gray that sprouted from my head, I'd become more aware that, biologically speaking, I was old enough to be their mother. So I didn't want to send their imaginations into overdrive with the evidence of a romantic evening etched onto my face.

And romance is what I had in mind.

Unlike my husband, I'd gone through some trouble with my appearance. I wore a red silk dress with a scalloped neckline to expose a tiny bit of cleavage, which, frankly, was all I had to display. I always envied women with expansive chests, women who could hide things between their breasts, like dollar bills or small children. Sadly, my boobs couldn't conceal a thing, but you work with you've got. So I had them trussed up as best I could in a black satin push-up bra. This was despite the efforts of the sales woman in the lingerie department who had, ever so gently, directed me away from the push-up bras, urging me toward staid beige foundational garments instead.

"Push-up bras are designed for more youthful figures," she whispered, eyes twinkling behind steel-rimmed granny glasses.

I resisted the urge to give her the youthful finger, shoved a big smile on my face, and bought a push-up bra anyway. Hell. Teenagers didn't need to lift and separate. In spite of their petite size, after nursing two daughters, my hard-working career breasts could use a boost.

My legs were my best asset, so I wore sheer black stockings with heels to show them off. I felt self-conscious about adding inches to my height, but David claimed it was one of the first things he was attracted to. Like having sex with a model he said, the first time we slept together in my dorm room on sweaty sheets, my legs straddling his, my head banging into the springs of the bunk above, opening a cut on my forehead that bled profusely while I came.

Underneath the stockings, I wore racy thong panties, which were not my usual thing. In fact, I felt pretentious in that underwear. I had always been a boy-short kind of girl. And although I fantasized about our evening, and I hoped for a resurgence of our old urgency, I was worried that the thong might seem silly, that David might laugh. But it was a chance I was willing to take, for David's birthday, for what I had come to think of as our new start.

A little rebranding couldn't hurt.

This evening was supposed to be all about us, to celebrate David's birthday and the completion of a grant proposal which purloined his attention for months. The girls were staying with his mother and we were going to enjoy a leisurely meal, then head home, where a bottle of champagne waited on ice. I'd have David build a fire to chase away the November chill, shimmy out of the red dress, and see what he thought of the thong.

David looked up from his menu and caught me staring at him. For a beat, the old electricity arced between us. Carnal knowledge held in the air like ozone, or pheromones, a little jolt to get the juices flowing.

But David frowned for some inexplicable reason and turned his attention to Chad. "New York strip, risotto, asparagus. Scotch, double."

Chad asked how he'd like his steak.

"Rare," said David. "Bloody."

Chad eyed me with a grin, before nodding and heading off, but David didn't seem to notice. He stirred in his seat and thumped his water glass, which emitted a dull ping. Cave-man style, I thought of David's order. David loved rare steak, but he knew I hated to watch him eat it. I rarely ate red meat myself, was close to being a vegetarian, though I made an obvious and important exception for bacon, which was, to my mind, its own food group.

David caught my look. "What's the problem?"

"Nothing."

He arched one brow.

"Okay, it's something. Bloody steak. Yuck."

"Jesus, Joanna. It's my birthday."

"Right. Of course."

There was no particular reason for David to care about my preferences when he ordered his meal, but it seemed more disgusting than usual, the idea of blood spurting from a hunk of barely cooked meat. Uncivilized. I pictured David feasting on the neck of a zebra, his bald spot exposed to the wandering eye of the African sun.

I shook my head to clear the bizarre image and saw Mike and Eleanor Radcliff about to pass our table. They didn't seem to notice us, and it was one of those awkward situations where you spy an acquaintance in public but you'd rather not chat. However, I knew if I didn't say hello I would have to avoid eye-contact with them for who knows how long in order to maintain the fiction that I hadn't seen them in the first place. I'm fully aware this might seem odd, to weigh the risks and benefits of a simple hello, but I choose to believe many people have such tendencies. After all, weren't Mike and Ellie walking past without saying hi to me?

With more force than necessary, I called out a cheery, "Mike, Eleanor, hello!"

Eleanor halted and Mike nearly plowed into her back, but side-stepped at the last instant to put a gentle hand at her waist. They swiveled as one to face us, smiling, in a well-executed waltz of glittering white teeth.

"Joanna, you look gorgeous," Eleanor said.

"Thanks Ellie, you too," I replied.

Eleanor, trim and petite, wore a tailored pink pant suit, with a helmet of black hair that was perfectly coiffed and unnatural in the way of a wig. Mike on the other hand was plump and badly bald, with an inch-wide circumference of silver hair cropped close to his skull. They were our next door neighbors, as well as David's colleagues at the University. Mike was chair of David's department and Eleanor some sort of administrator, Provost or Dean, I couldn't remember which.

"Is it a special occasion?" Eleanor asked.

"David's birthday," I said. "The big four-o."

Eleanor turned to David and smiled sweetly. "Goodness, I thought you were forty already."

"Kind of you." David raised his water glass in her direction.

"Not at all. I think it's wonderful that you're celebrating with your wife. You've hit a real milestone, haven't you? Or is it a fork in the road?"

"Some cliché or another," he said.

"A mid-life crisis?"

"It's just a birthday. I'm not at crisis stage yet."

"The water's still rising," said Eleanor.

"Or the bullshit's getting deeper," David replied.

Eleanor laughed softly, but there was a hard quality behind it.

"Let's go, Ellie, our table's ready," said Mike. He put a blunt hand on Eleanor's elbow and gave a slight tug. There was an ownership to the gesture that bespoke a long and successful alliance, one which didn't trade on silence and detachment. I wondered what those hands felt like in bed. Were they warm? Cool? Callused or smooth? Did Ellie welcome his touch?

"Enjoy your evening," Mike said.

"You should come by for drinks sometime," I replied.

Mike's hand gripped tighter on Eleanor's elbow, his loyal hand, while his lips stretched for an ill-fitting smile. Eleanor's eyes shone overly bright beneath crinkled violet eye-shadow.

"Sure Joanna," she said. "In fact, you and I should get together for coffee soon. Maybe next week? We can have a nice neighbor to neighbor chat."

And then they walked away.

David's eyes drilled a hole in her back and his hand clenched tight around his glass. I was conscious of some bitter missive passing through the air. It caused a tingling in my fingers, as if I could reach out and pluck it, like a rotting grape off the vine.

"That was strange," I said. "Don't you think that was kind of weird?"

"Eleanor's a bitch," he said flatly.

"David! She's our neighbor. What on earth is going on?"

"Oh nothing. It's just work stuff — IRB stuff."

Eleanor sat on the University Internal Review Board, which required endless paperwork for David to conduct experiments on human tissue explants.

"You've been butting heads with Eleanor?" I said.

"You could say that."

"Why?" I asked.

"I don't want to talk about it. I just want to eat my steak and get the hell out of here."

I flinched a little and made an enormous mental effort to let his remark bounce. It had nothing to do with me. He was only reacting to Eleanor.

Chad the waiter returned to our table carrying a tray. He placed the Scotch before David, laid out a basket of rolls, and shot an appreciative glance at my chest — which I confess, I did appreciate. At least someone had noticed the effects of the push-up bra.

David gripped his tumbler of amber liquid, and drank half in one swallow.

I shifted in my seat and felt the tug of thong underwear between my cheeks. I wanted to reach back and yank the string out of there, but that's where it was supposed to be, so I drained my glass of wine instead. If I was going to pull this off, the sexy underwear that is, I needed to be a little tanked.

I grabbed a roll, smeared it with dill butter, and stuffed a bite it in my mouth. I offered the bread basket to David but he shook his head no. Instead, he reached into his pocket and pulled out his phone. I suppressed a sigh and tried to think of something scintillating to say, something that would fascinate my husband as much as his smart phone. After the past few months, when our most consequential conversations dealt with bills and garbage day and laundry, I wanted to think of something pithy to say, some clever tidbit about the national debt or the North Korean nuclear threat or the new James Bond movie.

But I came up empty.

Meanwhile, David gazed into his tiny screen and caressed it with his thumbs like a lover.

A twenty-something couple occupied the booth across from us. The woman was lovely, blond, and plump, with manicured nails and abundant breasts spilling from a low cut lavender dress. The man across from her was big and soft-looking, an accountant or a banker, in a crisp button-down shirt. He ogled the woman adoringly. His cheeks were flushed, and a doltish smile played over his lips. A lone high-heeled pump languished on the floor beneath their table.

The woman had her foot in his lap.

A flush crawled up my cheeks. I felt like a voyeur, and then I felt jealous. How long had it been since David and I engaged in that sort of foreplay? Or had we ever? I couldn't remember.

Our sex life had gone missing, like a sock sucked into an alternate universe. I admit, at first I was relieved at the slower pace. It used to be a couple of nights a week, which seemed excessive after the girls came along. What mom couldn't use more sleep? But lately, I'd felt the lack. Marriage without sex was lonely. I guess that's how it ended up eventually, but we weren't there yet, were we? Anyway, I wasn't.

David had always worked long hours, but at the end of the day there was that connection between us. The act itself, sometimes hot, sometimes not, sometimes just there, the relief of sexual need, but also the luxury to touch and be touched. After all this time, the thought of unmarried sex seemed awkward to me: how to go about it, the condom issues, the self-consciousness of strangers. Married sex possessed a laziness that was comforting. One needn't hunt for it. It was right there in the bed beside you. Or it had been.

David was working harder than ever, putting long hours into his grant and pulling scientific research papers together. I taught an extra class the past semester, filling in for a colleague on maternity leave. And we juggled our daughters between us. We rarely had time together and when we did, we were too exhausted to do anything with it. Sex was collateral damage. But tonight I was determined to get things back on track. It was high time I got laid. So I pushed my heel off and eased my foot into David's lap.

He looked up from his phone, eyes wide.

My legs were long, so I had no trouble moving my foot between his thighs. I felt a hardening beneath my toes. I stroked up and down, with a mild buzz in my head. Relaxed, I thought. I was relaxed enough to give my husband a foot job in a restaurant. David blinked, his brows raised, but his penis seemed happy. I left my foot where it was, doing a little lap dance. Then I smiled at David, but he didn't smile back.

His phone buzzed on the table, and quickly, his penis went soft.

"Enough," he said, and threw a tense glance over his shoulder, like someone might see. Not so gently, he pushed my foot out of his lap. It dropped to the floor with a thud, throwing me off balance.

I righted myself and pushed my foot back into my shoe, trying to catch up with his shift in mood. "What was that for?"

"This isn't the time or place, Joanna."

"I thought you were into it," I said.

He shook his head and frowned. "I can't do this."

"Well, okay. Don't worry about it. PDAs aren't my usual thing either. But just wait until I get you home, Mister." I made a growling sound deep in my throat.

David ran his hands through his hair. "Joanna. You don't understand. I can't do this."

Disappointment washed through me. I could taste it, bitter and metallic, like old pennies. And something else, too: embarrassment racing into my head and neck with blood, like it had drained from David's penis straight into my face. David was a very private person. Of course he didn't want to get off in a restaurant. And I was a private person too. I'd never done this sort of thing before, because, honestly it wasn't my style. Still, there had been that spark, right? I hadn't imagined it. And there was his response at first, real and underfoot.

So what happened?

That's when the answer occurred to me, and it came as a wave of relief. David was turning forty. That wasn't old, really, but maybe he was having a physical issue, some kind of male menopause, prostate trouble perhaps?

I leaned toward him and spoke in a low voice. "Honey, is everything okay? Physically, I mean? Do you want me to make an appointment for you with Dr. Shelby?"

"Christ." He rolled his eyes.

"Sweetheart, it's just that it's been so long. You know? Maybe you need a little help. It's nothing to be ashamed of."

"What the hell are you talking about?" he asked, eyes narrowed.

"Maybe you need a prescription or something," I said. At some point, age gets the better of everyone, but it doesn't mean you have to give in to it, especially nowadays, when there are so many pharmaceutical solutions.

"A prescription?"

"They have pills, to help — you know, with sex."

"Are you kidding? I don't need any fucking blue pills, Joanna," he hissed.

"David, don't swear."

Chad the waiter showed up bearing a tray of food. I twisted my scratched gold wedding band and diamond solitaire as Chad arranged the plates artfully before us. He asked if we needed anything else.

"Another Scotch," said David, tapping his glass, with a hard look in my direction.

"Chablis for me," I said, wishing to drown out David's disapproval.

"Of course," said Chad. He took the opportunity to wink at me while

David unfolded his napkin, and I suppressed a bubble of manic mirth as he swaggered away to place our order at the bar. There he stopped to chat with an attractive and vaguely familiar young black woman, who sat high astride a leather bar stool. Chad was nothing if not dedicated to his job.

David pressed his lips together and shook his head. He began to saw through his steak. Blood oozed out of it and made a glistening moat around the risotto. The muscular aroma, at once charred and underdone, triggered another vulgar vision of David gnawing at a carcass in the sun, with hyenas laughing all around, awaiting their turn at the tasty treat.

Nausea curled in my stomach.

David said, "What's gotten into you?"

He speared a grim looking bite, tucked it into his mouth, and dabbed at his lips with a linen napkin — the debonair Neanderthal. He looked at me expectantly.

Finally, I had his attention. But what should I say? I couldn't bear to watch him chew, so I raked through the linguine with my fork. I poked at the clams, tiny creatures that kept their mouths shut for their entire lives, delicate flesh now exposed in a silent scream. I avoided the shellfish, forked up some linguini, and began to shovel it into my mouth. But my fingers twitched and I dropped the fork, which clattered onto my plate.

I fixed David with a stare, and I saw his face, lined but still handsome, still dear to me, superimposed on the face of a younger man, the man I met at Duke University fifteen years ago, working on his PhD in biochemistry, a young man who loved me.

"I want to know what's going on," I said. "Something's different."

He stared back at me but didn't say a word.

"Something's changed, David," I said. "I don't know if it's some problem you're having, or if it's something I've done, or if we're just too busy. But remember how it used to be? I used to read to you in bed? Remember that? We'd make love and you'd fall asleep with your hand on my stomach. I want that again. That's all, David. I want you again."

He still didn't say anything, but gazed over my shoulder with a far-off look in his eye. Then he sighed and said, "Oh Jo, just eat, okay?"

I sat there a moment, stunned. Well, fuck it then. I'd eat. I grabbed my fork and pried the meat from a clamshell, and my fingers began tingling, the sensation shooting up my trembling arms, down into my abdomen, and coalescing behind my eyes.

I ate as much as I could stomach and downed another glass of wine. We didn't order dessert. And after an unbearably long time, David's birthday dinner was done. It seemed absurd now that I had wanted to celebrate. He paid the bill, and I threw Chad a smoldering glance. Why the hell not? As we stood to leave, David grabbed me by the elbow, but I pulled free and strode out ahead of him, past the booths filled with customers and the woman at the bar, whose phone sat next to an empty cocktail. Her head of spiral curls swiveled to watch our progress, no doubt drawn by the air of disaster.

We weaved out the door and into the November night. My ridiculous heels clicked on brick pavers littered with fallen leaves, plastic cups, and cigarette butts, detritus from the home game football crowd. A clump of drunken college students hovered at a bench in front of the restaurant, talking, smoking, laughing, the smell of beer and cigarettes pungent in the near-winter air. They were a blur, indistinguishable from each other, enviable and carefree in their self-immolation, naïve to the burdens of mortality, the shortening of time and dreams gone by. In the way of children and drunks, they were impervious to the cold, dressed in jeans, t-shirts, and short skirts, as they clutched at each other, the sex between them no doubt easy and interchangeable.

When the students were safely behind us, I stepped in front of David.

"What now?" he asked.

"Let's play twenty questions, all right? I ask and you answer. I deserve that much of your time."

David's face was washed out in the streetlight, tired. Undoubtedly, I looked the same.

"Are you gay?" I asked.

He snorted a blast of frozen air into the night.

"Are you having some kind of sexual problem?"

"We covered that already," he said. "No."

"Do you love me?"

For the first time, I saw something like pain cross his face.

After a moment, he nodded yes.

"Are you in love with me?"

He ran a hand through his hair. "I wish — I wish I could say I was."

I stood there, and an agonizing blankness swallowed me. I was cold and numb. But I started this game and now I had to finish it.

"Are you in love with someone else?" I whispered.

He hesitated a second and then said, "Yes."

I stepped back from him as if I could avoid absorbing the answer, as if it were a toxic and miscible substance. I shivered spasmodically, like a lab mouse succumbing to carbon dioxide.

"Who?" I managed to ask.

He gulped, apparently struck dumb by the question. And that's when she walked out of the restaurant, the woman from the bar, in a leather jacket, belted above bare legs, which came scissoring toward us now, proud and purposeful. The woman drew closer, with luscious lips and bitter chocolate eyes, and I realized, with the dull and stupid surprise of the slowly poisoned, that this was, in fact, someone I knew. Someone I'd seen in different circumstances, much more primly dressed, in a lab coat, in David's lab. The woman stumbled and swerved toward us, then grabbed David's arm for balance. She shot me a grin, bold and predatory.

David blinked rapidly, and held onto the woman, preventing her spill to the pavement. She stood on tip-toe to kiss his cheek, pressing her breasts against him, and sent a smirk in my direction. *You don't mind, do you?*

"Happy birthday, Professor," she purred.

David's eyes flicked between us. His mouth worked, trying to find a suitable sentiment for the situation, I suppose, before settling into a gross approximation of a smile, as if he were the host of this dreadful little party.

"Joanna —" he began, and fell into a hacking cough, overcome, perhaps, by some squall of shame, or regret, or both — which soon passed. For when the spell was done, he stood upright, composed his face in solemn arrangement, fit for the eulogy of a marriage, and wrapped his arms more firmly around her.

"Joanna," he uttered again. "You remember my student?"

Of course I did. Celeste. It was Celeste.

Gabriel Knipp
The Yellow Candle

I have started six forest fires. The longest burned for 23 days, like the psalm. That fire happened in Idaho, after I watched myself start it, trembling, during a hailstorm. The hail recoiled off of my shoulders; I leaned over so it could not see what I did. I used a match and dry pine needles that rattled in my hand. Dirt stained my fingernails. Later, I saw on TV that three firemen died. They were all men because that's what the news said. No one else ever died in my fires, even when I prayed that someone would. Every other fire burned less than a week. My first, third, and fourth fires lived less than a day. I don't know why I kept at it.

Once, I was at an ice cream shop in Buena Vista — that's a Spanish word, but everyone has forgotten this — and saw a photo of the suspect in the Colorado fire. That's a Spanish word, too. The suspect was a man; they always think it is a man. Everyone suspects a man only because they think fire is hot and angry, but it is spirit and sacrifice, like a woman.

➤

But now they are watching me.

➤

My brother went to Utah first. The wilderness was meant to change him, until a drunk driver collided with his van, but the drunk drove a Corolla so everyone walked away; they just had to wait on the side of the road while the drunk sobbed alongside them, while the drunk stank of piss, while the drunk cussed at the car. The drunk was a woman, but you probably thought it was a man because 97% of drunk drivers are men. After that, my parents brought my brother home but trauma did not change their plan to send me; we must have passed each other on the highway, unnoticed.
They say religion began in the desert: there is only rock and sun and either you hear God or invent God.

My first fire happened in the desert when Lucy did not return her lighter after the smoke break. At night, they tied our shoes and kept them in the counselor's tent so no one could run; when you went to the bathroom you had to ring a bell the entire time or they would come after you; the continuous shaking always ensured piss dripped onto your thigh, your shoes. But

Lucy kept the lighter after smoke break when Tomi disappeared — Tomi is a boy's name, too, even when it has an "i", and Tomi liked to wrestle — and the counselor chased after her and we all had to go inside our squalid tents. After dark, Lucy touched my fingertips so I opened my hand; she placed the lighter there. I slid out of our tent and sat, for a moment, next to the counselor's tent; I could hear their deliberate breathing. Time does not turn in the desert; past and future are imaginary. Dirt stained my fingernails, then, too; I saw it when I flicked the lighter next to their polyester fly. The fire burned bright and green. I prayed they might die. Robert cussed as he tried to crawl out but couldn't get the door unzipped, his voice full of gravel and sleep, and then Jason bowled out, still wrapped in his sleeping bag. I stood with the lighter tight in my hand like a fish, firm and careful; later Lucy told me I was smiling. Our shoes burned, and Robert's jacket, and the prescription medication each of us took in the morning. Without our meds, no one knew what time it was. They had to call for help and then couldn't find the road; we spent the next day and night wandering the desert, unsure of what time it was. They sent me home three weeks later because I was functional again. I didn't know what that meant. I was sixteen.

I see a pickup, framed by the translucent window of my tent. A man with a beard, maybe 100 yards away, whistles as he walks to the creek. He glances at my tent six times.

My brother's name is Mason, which everyone uses for a girl's name now, but it began as a boy's name — before everyone forgot. We shared a room until I turned nine and we moved into a house with four bedrooms; we didn't even need to use one, but my mom said she read in it at night after Dad went to sleep. We were all happy at that house. Sometimes, I slunk over to Mason's room in the small, tranquil hours and we whispered about how many psalms we could recite. They were badges of courage: my mother forced us to memorize them as punishments if we spoke back or did not eat all of our dinners. I think of one whenever I light a fire. I suppose I am God, the fire at my fingertips, my breath shallow and anxious, the flame ready to roll on the wind. I am God.

My second fire happened in Utah, too. We lived in a trailer park then; we moved after my dad was laid off when I was 11. My mom cried when the movers took their bed apart. Mason and I didn't recite our psalms together anymore; it felt childish, and though we could remember them — we could always remember them — we shoved them into the back of our dresser drawers where you put things you either love or want to keep so secret that even you forget them. My mom stopped at the neighbor's trailer each night when she came home from work, and my dad read through the entire encyclopedia that year. He shaved his beard, too. He used to tickle my tummy with it when I was young.

But before my family broke in, I was going to tell you about the second fire. I had turned nineteen and my mom threatened to kick me out of the trailer; I took her car and her jar of tips and drove west to where I had been three years earlier, except I reached the red hills that we had always been straining toward. I didn't know what I was going to do until it was night and I snaked through the hills; the fire I started three years ago still burned in my head — our shoes in the flames. I pulled over and stood in the coolness next to a scrub pine. Juniper bushes spread irregularly across the slopes. I kicked together some pine needles and had a match, because it was my mom's car. I lit one and watched the flame burn down, almost to my fingertips to where it hurt. I dropped it and the match blew out.

People don't drop matches to light fires like in the movies. Instead, they stop thinking. Time is neither past nor future. All they see is the match, feel the pull of the pine needles and imagine the release of the fire. There is only fire and pain, both if the flame touches the needles. Then it does and your fingernails are dirty, but you can feel the heat on the palms of your hands. The flames flash six inches, then a foot. The fire has burned for no time, yet you don't remember what it was like before it was lit. The flames rise to two feet, three feet high and the heat reaches your face. You made this out of nothing. There is light and heat and you, and the flames consume a pine tree; they grow so loud and large that you are afraid. You run to the car and the wind blows the fire east so you drive west, sweating and breathless, heat still on your skin, the fire in the mirror.

I had breakfast in Bend, Oregon, and slept after in the stuffy green heat of a tent I had bought from an Army Surplus store. The next day, I ate breakfast at the same café and saw the Utah fire in the paper. I drove out to the hills and tried to start another one, in the middle of the day because I didn't know what else to do. The sweat made my hair stick to my cheeks and forehead; I kept wiping the wet hair away from my eyes. It burned for half an hour before the wind changed and it died. It was not the same as my first two; I lit it because I could, not because I needed the fire. I sold my car to a man who lived in a school bus after that, so I had to work for my fires, to really love them. I bought a paper, too, which had said that what happened in Utah could happen there. The paper.

After the man glances at my tent six times, I pack slowly and deliberately, like I have nothing to hide. He walks back to his pickup and waves; I smile and wave back. I try not to smile too big so he comes over. I wonder what I should do if he does, if I should run or pretend to talk to him, but he doesn't come. I pack the tent and walk out along the creek, along fragmented boulders and intricate tree roots. There's a gravel road, but the man might come down it and talk to me; it's safer to walk along the creek.

My fourth fire happened in New Mexico. It started upwind from a little adobe Catholic church. It was a shrine, I think, outside of Santa Fe. That's another Spanish word. I thought of the psalms that my mother forced upon us and how it took faith to believe that I was a God, that I could bring this fire into existence. I started that one with the newspaper from Bend, the very section that said Oregon was in danger of a fire. I used matches from our house, they said *Deltas* on them with no apostrophe. It was the restaurant where my mom worked. I lit the newspaper under a Juniper bush and the bush burned like paper, too. Soon, I saw a priest outside on a cell phone, his cassock swaying; he stood under the front porch lamp in a circle of light. I actually prayed the fire wouldn't burn down the church, even though I had lit it, even though I loved it. The fire department came and soaked the church and the Juniper bushes around it; the fire blackened the steeple but did not burn the church down. I didn't know if it was a miracle, or if it counted because the fire department came, destroying all faith.

After that, I took a bus back home and found Mason in bed with a girl I knew from high school. He swore at me and I told him I would burn his house down. Our house. Our trailer. "Dad killed himself," he said. Then he said it again. His face was shiny, stubbled. He caught me when I fell to the ground and held me; his fan turned lazily in the breeze. "I should never have left," I said. "He used sleeping pills and Tylenol," said Mason. "I should never have left," I told him. I didn't notice when the girl left. Mason's stubble was sharp on my cheek, not soft like my father's beard was. Not yet.

"Where can I say goodbye?"

"He was cremated. He's in mom's room."

"What does it look like?"

"What?"

"The urn."

"It's black, I guess. Shiny."

I pictured it, sitting forgotten on a dresser.

Mason gave me $232 dollars, which he had been saving for a new car, but said it was okay. Before I left, he confided he had stolen it all from Mom. The drunk. My face was tight from crying when I left, and I could hear Mom in the other room. It was night.

That was fifteen months ago. I remember wondering if my father was some spirit, and if I would ever know he was near, and if he would ever help me if I needed.

I ride in the back of a pickup to a gas station, next to a mutt-dog. The driver, a woman, glances incessantly in the rearview mirror, so I lie down and stare at the sky. There are no clouds. At the gas station where she leaves me, the fathers walk by in their sneakers and the mothers in their eyeliner.

You cannot hear anyone watching you in the city, not like the wilderness. A Middle Eastern man comes and tells me to leave. I wonder if my father is watching, and why he chose sleeping pills and Tylenol.

My fifth fire was the Idaho fire and it burned for twenty three days. I thought it would never stop; it would burn up the whole world. That was the one I started in the hailstorm when heaven itself was breaking apart and my fingernails had stains on them. I felt so dizzy after lighting the fire that I lay down, the accumulated hail cold on my back, the flames raging and hot. I had singed the fingertip of my right index finger because I held onto the match too long; it hurt for two weeks. The fire grew so large so quickly that I cussed at God and shivered. The flames clapped against the sky like they could beat it down. I see the flames, nothing for a moment and then exploding with the wind, then nothing again until they scorch a pine; I felt so afraid: it was beautiful. They are mystery and hate, and I am their God.

It is hard to breathe when the fires are burning, or when I think of them burning. I love them. I love them.

In the Idaho fire three firemen died. Sometimes I think about their families. I wonder if the men loved their wives and what they thought about when the fires rolled at them, hot and bright; if they embraced the fire, unafraid, or shrank away. I think if you are unafraid you must go to heaven, because you didn't love this life too much. And heaven must not be too bad a place.

The news anchor said the fire was 200 meters from a town — I don't know why he said meters — and I wanted that town to burn: the shops and cars and houses. I wanted the houses to burn. But the three firemen died and stopped the fire and everyone slept in their own rooms two nights later. I wonder if the firemen knew they would save the town; I wonder if it was beautiful, somehow. I didn't want anyone to die. I didn't want them to die.

There is a Catholic church 12 minutes from the gas station and I walk to it. I don't know why I do this, some unconscious yearning. Or perhaps, it is penance. I cross myself at the door to the Catholic church, since that it what I have seen others do. There are a few old ladies dispersed about the pews and a dying Jesus in front of everyone. His hair and body are carved from wood. He wears a loincloth, but I know, in truth, he was naked and everybody could see him: nothing between God and the world. I genuflect and sit down and wonder if Jesus' skin turned purplish and pimpled, if it was cold on the cross, and if he didn't want the people to watch him and write about him because now the world couldn't stop talking about what they wanted him to be. The old ladies and young boy who walks in alongside his mother: they abduct Jesus and use him for themselves. Even I do, sitting on the hard, wooden bench that would burn with a fury. But only the fires bring relief.

My last fire was in Colorado and I waited 13 months and nine days since the men had died and I did not want anyone else to die, ever. But I had to light it. We are all made to do something, and I was made to light fires. Still, I hated myself after that. I hated when they said it was arson. Arson does not describe the cackle and snap of a fire. A fire demands a word with some sibilance, something onomatopoetic. All our words are only half-true. The fire in Colorado burned for six days until they put it out, and now the news anchor with the dark hair says they have a suspect. That was to throw me off and make me forget that they are watching. Jesus stares up at heaven and I sit there and pray that everything might become real — all the words to the psalms my mother forced us to memorize. The Lord is my shepherd, I shall not want. More people enter the church, a father and his young daughter, Hispanic. I shall not want, I whisper, thinking only of the fires. I shall not want this life. I shall be unafraid.

A priest walks out, his cassock swaying. I leave before Mass begins, a tremor in my fingers. Outside, I laugh because I prayed but maybe words are formless and void, signifying nothing. I laugh because I am scared of what may happen.

It is nothing I say to myself and there are two blond boys on a bus bench, watching me, and one of them asks, "What is nothing?" and they both laugh. I wonder if the boys look like the young men who died. They all died on June 21, which is the longest day of the year, but perhaps they couldn't even see the sun and did not know. I wonder if their wives are lonely and drunk now, or if they had daughters. I glance over my shoulder and the blond boys still watch me like I am on parade, like they can, for an instant, see me. I push out my chest so they will see me for what I am not. When you light a fire everything is real. There is a park and a man with a beard holds a toddler. There is a woman with a swollen belly. I try to think if maybe he is the man from the creek; I don't remember him exactly. My father used to always tell me I needed to think about what I was looking at, but when you can feel a fire, you cannot think. It had to be the man from the creek, so I start running. I run toward my house even though I am afraid. My father had a beard before he killed himself. No. Did he? He will help me anyway. He will help me or nothing matters anyway.

The man with a beard is near the sidewalk and he throws his arms out to a toddler and says, "Come here." He glances at me when he says it because I am running in the city. I run as fast as I can like I can drift into the sky and disappear; my feet are light and my lungs hot; my ponytail drags behind me. The park ends but the man with the beard still says "Come here," and he is looking at me, two blocks back, Come here, come here, and I dash into the street because he won't stop watching me; I don't want anyone to see me and he can.

The car's brakes shriek like an animal. Then, only the horn sounds, low and deep like a judge, low and deep like a judge. Everyone looks at me, even the people in the park, the horn accusing me. The driver has a beard, I think. The horn continues but the car has stopped so I run faster, like there is no earth, toward home. Everyone watches me even though I cannot see them, and I wonder if anyone sees me or if they only watch a spectacle.

It is dusk when I tap on Mason's window but I hear nothing. My finger still trembles but I tap again. He leaves his window unlocked, always, and there is no screen so I slide it open. It whines as I do, and our trailer is so small, and the shrill penetrates it like smoke, through the thin walls and cracks under the door. I grunt as I climb in, too, because I have to lift without using my feet. I bump the fan on the table; it wobbles but does not fall. Thank God.

My breath will not come to me. The floor creaks so I sit on the bed, staring out the window while darkness descends from the clouds. I am patient — I learned it in the wilderness — but it is like I'm already breathing smoke. Children laugh outside and bounce a ball; I hear a boy cuss but he is too young; I must go out and tell him not to do that, not to do that because he is too young and his father might take sleeping pills and Tylenol if he does it too much, but I just sit there on Mason's unmade bed. A photo of the two of us rests on his dresser beside a yellow candle. I have heard nothing outside his door, but I can hear nothing above the sharp staccato sound of my breath. I cross the hall into my old room, the one I used for a few years after my dad lost his job. Before I ran away.

The room still smells like me, somehow, like my dirty hair and the faint stench of old incense, and I can even smell it through my mouth. The bed is gone, sold or given away, replaced by a desk with a Bible and disorganized bills. I open the closet and it has five file cabinets and a yellow hooded sweatshirt that I wore in high school and I put it on but it is immediately too hot, except I can't take it off.

I peek out the front door to see the mobile home where my mother used to go when it was dark.

My chest rises as I take the yellow candle from Mason's room. I open my dresser, the top drawer. It is filled with papers now, like my mother cannot have enough papers around her, enough ones and zeroes, enough words to make her forget; only no one can ever forget because time is always connected to itself, and we would not be if we forgot; we would not be. Taped to the back of the drawer, where no one ever looks and where you can only reach if you pull the drawer out halfway and your wrists are small, like a woman's, is an envelope. I take it, and the yellow candle, to my parents' — my mother's — room. I breathe deep not because I need to but to remain unafraid. "Daddy," I say.

There are no photographs of us in my mother's room, and I open the envelope; we are standing in front of a Catholic church in Santa Fe and smiling; Dad had just been laid off and had a job interview, everything shone with anticipation so he took the whole family for vacation. We are all squinting, Dad with his beard and his hand up to his forehead to block the sun, Mom with a pale ring-less hand on Mason's shoulder, Mason in a black t-shirt and the black hair on his upper lip visible. Me. My hair is down and looks auburn in the light. We moved to the trailer four months later.

There is a box of matches in the envelope from a restaurant where we dined, which was built from an old railroad depot, and Dad told me the line used to run from Santa Fe to a mile away from our house. That was before we moved and before automobiles and internet and before Dad took the pills and before I struck a match maybe ever. Peppers hung above the tables and we all tried one. Mason laughed because of how my eyes watered. My mouth felt like it was on fire and Dad left the table to get a glass of milk for me and then left his hand on my shoulder while I drank it.

I can't breathe but it doesn't matter. The curtains on my mother's window are gauzy, like clouds. I look through to the other trailer where she goes and I see the same old man from the creek disappear around the corner of a trailer three spaces down. I swear. I hope it is him. But I do not know anything; I see things and have always seen things so Dad always told me to see what I'm looking at.

"Save me," I say.

The match is nothing, then blue, then yellow. I put it to the yellow candle. I cannot think, now; I can only feel because a fire is burning. I cough; my lungs cannot find enough air and I am gasping. It is hot in my sweatshirt, but I see my father across the room in the urn, the black urn; it is cold on my fingertips when I touch it. He is in the black polished urn, his hand and his beard, all of him, all of him, all of his ashes. Words are nothing but he tickled my tummy when I was small, tickled it with his beard, and time will not let me forget. It always is.

I cross the hall into Mason's room and take the window fan back to my parents' room. Its hum is unnatural, but the breeze makes the hair on the back of my neck stand up from the sweat. It is so hot. I blow the fan along the wall, past the gauze curtains and toward my old room where there are only papers now, and bills.

I hold my breath and then gasp, and gasp, and gasp; the fan blows my own hair into my face and I wonder if anyone will see me. I cannot catch my breath; I have been gasping all my life save the time Dad gave me that glass of milk, save that time but I can't catch my breath now and there is fire in my shoulder blades because I can't breathe and I'm dizzy, so dizzy, so dizzy, but I can stand enough to take the candle over to the gauze curtain which is like a cloud and shakes because I gasp. I gasp. I gasp.

I take the urn, cool for the moment. My fingernails are dirty. The flame is yellow against the gauze curtains, bright yellow, and they burn like paper.

The smoke is black, already shadowing the room, but the fire is so, so bright.

My name is Faith, I forgot to say.

I lie downwind from the flames, between the clouds and my room, and the urn is at my chest and the photo is on the floor before my face: all of us smiling, right before Dad put his hand on my shoulder at the restaurant. The urn is warm now. The wind blows on me, and then I feel the heat. I wonder about the man with the beard, and my father, and my hair blows in front of my eyes.

Nonfiction

Eugene Durante

A Tale of Stop (And Not) Frisk

I'm on a Manhattan bound train staring out the window as it leaves Brighton Beach. The train is nearly empty after midnight, and I'm positioned by the door in what would, over the years, become my "patrol stance" — standing sideways, facing the length of the car, right elbow resting on my firearm, and left boot heel wedged into the door partition.

I'm on the left side of the train as it lurches northbound picking up passengers either en route to a night shift, or a New York night out. The crisp air rushes in the door at every stop as I embrace the silent effect of the late night/cold weather radio. With exactly one year on the job, I haven't yet learned how the best crime fighting efforts are not attributed to police brass or politicians, but rather the cold and rainy tendencies of mother nature.

My assignment to late night train patrol was precipitated earlier that winter by a 'lush worker.' He was cutting open the pockets of sleeping passengers to remove personal items while they slept. The crime was not atypical for the hour or area, and the perpetrator's description from eyewitness accounts was a black male, 18 – 30 years old, wearing a black jacket, black pants, and armed with a box cutter. My platoon had been briefed numerous times about the robbery pattern, and with rookie ambition we certainly contributed our share of the stop and frisk reports generated that year by the NYPD.

As the train pulled into the Neck Road station, I noticed an unusual figure across the way. He furtively moved on the Coney Island platform. His back was towards me, but in just a few seconds I had him locked in my vision. He was a tall black male with braided hair. He wore a full length black jacket and black pants. His hands were in front of him, and he was awkwardly walking left to right while facing the wall. I could not tell if he was kicking the wall, marking it with paint, or moving back and forth while urinating. I quickly sprung from my leaning position and off the train.

Utilizing the advice of veteran train patrol officers, I tactically stepped out of view, down a few exit stairs, and surveyed the cloaked figure. Fortunately, his train had also just left, and I knew I had plenty of observation time before I would move in. His behavior persisted, so I crossed over for a closer look. While sneaking up the far staircase on his side, I made a common rookie mistake.

My radio had come screeching alive, and I quickly muffled it with my hands. The male froze, then looked around. I was surprised he picked up the noise from that distance, but Neck Road is an eerily silent and creepy place late at night. Prior to renovation, the station was a spawning ground for rats and pigeons. Even today, there isn't enough revenue to justify staffing the token booth after sunset.

Broad shouldered, the curious figure turned my way and stood silent as I slowly approached. His hands were at his sides, and his fingers were spread apart. He looked about 40 years old from the sporadic gray hair at the base of his braids. I sensed he was no stranger to being stopped by the police.

"How you doing?," I casually stated, utilizing a common New York greeting.

"I'm lost," he said, "I fell asleep on the train."

Getting closer, I noticed his black dress shoes and black suit beneath the trench coat, and I let my guard down a bit.

"Must have been a good sleep," I said, "You've drooled on yourself."

He started wiping his outer coat with a handkerchief as he awkwardly looked away and not at the stain as most people would. Then I noticed his walking stick and backpack on the floor next to the garbage pail.

"I know my home station perfectly," he said, gathering his articles, "but I have no idea where I am now. Thank you very much for being here."

"Just check your belongings, sir. Unattended items grow legs quickly in Brooklyn. These scummers will steal your walking stick if you don't pay attention."

He smiled, and with that we broke the ice.

Escorting the gentleman to the other platform, he quickly reminded me of a forgotten lesson from the police academy, *let the blind person grab your arm for better guidance.* We exchanged names as I led him back to a bench and awaited the next train.

He asked how long I was on the job. I replied, and I then inquired if he was born blind or lost his vision over time.

"I lost my sight in the last decade, but I can still see silhouettes," he said.

"That's very fortunate," I encouraged.

"Sometimes I wish I never had vision though," he said while adjusting his long coat in the seat. "I think I'd have less anxiety overall."

Not understanding his point, he went on to explain. ...

"Instead of becoming a man and earning my independence in the world, I have to live with my mother and sister for support. I'm blessed that I still have family, but I always dreamed of moving out of the ghetto after college. It's sad enough that I've changed, but I have witnessed myself become a different person to others. To the outside world I've become a 'He,' as in, would 'He' like a chair or a booth, or would 'He' like another cup of coffee ... as if *I* never existed."

His voice cracked a bit now, "You have no idea what it feels like when I go shopping and I ask the salesman if a shirt is a light or darker tone of black, and he answers me, 'Does it really matter?'"

"You know, I used to always date hot women, and now I'm alone. Heck, I don't even know what the Spice Girls look like!"

Becoming reflective for a moment, the blind man stared toward the darkness saying nothing. Then the rattle of a train in the distance started vibrating the tracks. We boarded the next train together arm in arm to his home station. On our way, we discussed our experiences growing up in Brooklyn and how the city was changing. Stepping off the train, he softly pushed my arm away. "I got this," he said, and he breezed up the stairs and out to street level in no time. I offered to walk him home, but he insisted I should not.

"I understand. We both have reputations to protect in these parts," I joked. We extended a meaningful handshake and that half-a-hug gesture that men do so well.

"Hey, Durante," he said, "Thanks again for being there, and more importantly, thank you for treating me like a regular guy."

I watched him walk away as my rookie radio reverberated off the walk-up buildings along Marlborough Road.

Looking back, I recognize how poignant the compliment was. Although I do not remember his name, a heartfelt compliment was a rare experience prior to September 11th. As police officers, we're conditioned to think our careers are defined by newsworthy events, but too often we overlook the touching moments that help us become better cops and better human beings.

Kristine Langley Mahler

Art Alexakis

You were sitting on a curb on the 'Bash next to Art Alexakis, and you couldn't believe you were where you were. He wasn't the REAL Art Alexakis from Everclear, but he looked like him, on the back cover of "So Much for the Afterglow," with his bleached short hair and dark eyebrows, and the little bit of dark facial stubble brushed across his mouth and chin, and that's why you were bothering to have a crush on him. No, you were bothering to have a crush on him because he recognized the back of your head at the orientation for Summer Honors camp, and you were like *the back of my* HEAD? And he said, "Yeah, me and my friends know you by the back of your head." You were strangely flattered — you could be picked out of a crowd by someone you'd never met who didn't even know you by your face?

"Well, I don't recognize the back of YOUR head," you flirted back at Art. "That's because you're not walking behind me," he said and leaned back in his chair, grinning. Who was this guy and how had he escaped sharing classes with you for the last three years? He was at Summer Honors camp doing the pre-med track, so he was obviously SMART. There were about sixty kids in your grade who shuffled between the two honors versions of every class offered, and you already knew who you'd see each semester — and you'd never seen him. You felt like you'd just discovered a hidden treasure: a smart guy in your grade, in your school, that the other girls in your track didn't seem to know about.

You were uncharacteristically sassy that summer — you and three other girls in your writing camp gave each other ridiculous gangster names like "Prison Bitch" and "Ghetto Snatch." You were "Gutter Pimp," borrowing Trailer Whore's punked-out green Doc Martens and wearing a black Gothic cross dress to the all-camp dance, swanning around the girls' dormitory, talking shit in the hallway in your cargo shorts and bra because you didn't give a fuck; these weren't girls who were going to tease you in REGULAR LIFE when you got back to high school in the fall. No one was shocked by Honors-Class Girl acting like a gutter punk because no one KNEW you as Honors-Class Girl. It made you excited about real college, made you realize you'd get to shake off the social confines dictating who you must be based on who you'd been.

Near the end of camp, you ran into Art by the fountain near the student union, and when he asked what you were doing the rest of the summer, you told him you were going on a two-week trip to the East Coast with your family. He said, "You want to go for a walk?" so you two wandered between the buildings, heat lightning shocking through the trees. It started sprinkling, and you two hurried under a tree, under the leaves, and you were so convinced he was going to kiss you that you were storing away the entire scenario in your mind so you could describe it to your girls back at the dorm, but he didn't.

As you got to your dorm, Art asked when you'd be back from your trip, asked for your phone number, and called you the day you got home. You were shocked that he was THAT interested in you; you and Art talked on the phone for the next three nights, casually flirting, but not really saying anything important, not really getting to know each other. He asked if you wanted to hang out on Friday night and you were like SURE.

On Friday night, Art arrived at your house with a friend already in the front seat of Art's Crown Victoria, which looked like a former police car, so you reluctantly opened the door to the backseat and sat there by yourself. You three headed off into the night, out of your suburban neighborhood on the outskirts of town into the heart of your city. Art said he had to stop at his house for a minute and as he turned onto a side street you sucked in your breath, startled. His house resembled the small ranch house you'd lived in when you were getting free lunches at elementary school; three subsequent moves and three larger houses later, you weren't exactly PICKY about that sort of thing, it just surprised you.

Art led you through the vinyl front door and you stood beside the plastic-covered sofa as Art's friend walked back to the telephone in the kitchen, talking to Art's older sister, who was pregnant as hell, and was also the Winter Homecoming Queen from two years ago. You suddenly remembered that Art was her brother, and it also suddenly depressed you that a girl could go from wearing an ermine-trimmed robe and posing for the portrait that would hang with all the other Queens from the last three decades on the wall outside the Principal's office, to winding up here, pregnant and still living at home with her parents, the baby's daddy nowhere in sight. You thought a Homecoming Queen was destined for greatness.

Art's friend hollered from the kitchen that a couple of boys with two names which you instantly forgot were going to the 'Bash, and you all headed out to Art's Crown Vic again.

As Art drove north, you couldn't believe where you were heading. The 'Bash was the main road in your town; well, it USED to be the main road in town back when people actually used to go downtown. But for years the 'Bash had been littered with awful closed storefronts and no one went to the 'Bash except for one reason: to cruise.

It had been a subject of ridicule among your friends for as long as you'd been in your town. The rednecks and white trash would slowly drive up and down a two-mile-long strip of the 'Bash, checking out who was parked alongside the street, who was hanging out in the back of whose Dodge Ram, or who was surreptitiously stashing their cans of beer behind the tires.

No one who was ANYONE cruised the 'Bash. "Cruising the 'Bash" was a phrase you'd bandy about with your friends, an Option C for bored Friday nights that you'd never actually choose; you'd rather go home than be caught on that road after 8 PM It was a lame joke, a pathetic excuse for the kids from the country to come into town. You could go to Kroger, or you could go to Rally's, or you could go to Walgreen's, but the rest of the 'Bash was nothing, decades-dead storefronts exposed by broken-glass windows.

So, as Art drove to the 'Bash, you were torn between wanting to invent an excuse to make him take you home early and wanting to see the scene. As he began the crawl along the 'Bash, it dawned on you that you wouldn't see a single person you knew along the 'Bash. No one with a decent reputation would be there, no one from your classes — frankly, no one from your class. Your SOCIAL class. So you took a deep breath, shrugged your shoulders, and surrendered to the WT experience: bowl-cut farmer boys wearing t-shirts with the sleeves ripped off at the shoulders, blasting Garth Brooks, tapered jeans, cowboy boots. And white trash boys in their trashy Metallica t-shirts from concerts they never went to, greased-back blond ponytails, white trash girls in high-waisted, ill-fitting TIGHT short skirts, platform shoes, smoking cigarettes and hanging on the boys or standing with their arms crossed, glaring.

You had thrown around the term "white trash" before; you didn't think it meant anything other than people from a lower socioeconomic class than yours, and you called them white trash, or WT, without a second thought. You never thought about the implication that other races were implicated as straight-up TRASH.

When Art parked the car on the 'Bash in front of the Walgreen's that your best friend's mom had come to forcibly stop her from working at on her second day of employment because "it was in a bad neighborhood," you took another deep breath and got out of the car, sitting on the curb next to Art. You didn't know what you were supposed to talk to him about now. How you'd never cruised the 'Bash before? You had an inclination he already knew that. You didn't know anyone there so you couldn't start talking about someone you saw down the street. But then Art started talking to you, a conversation that started like it was something you two had been talking about before, how he still talked to his old girlfriend Allison a lot, how he didn't know why they'd broken up.

You were about one second away from leaping up and stamping your feet on the curb, your arms flung up into the air, screaming that YOU COULDN'T BELIEVE THIS WAS HAPPENING TO YOU. What the FUCK? Why the SHIT were you sitting on a curb on THE FUCKING 'BASH with this guy who wasn't even treating you like a potential girlfriend, who was talking to you like you were a GUY, like you could RELATE?

But something in you snapped into place, and you decided to just listen; Art Alexakis wasn't EXPLICITLY saying he wanted to get back together with her. Maybe he was testing to see how you'd react to hearing about another girl. So you didn't exactly tell him to try to hook up with her again, but you also didn't act jealous.

When Art and his friend drove you home that night to make your eleven-o'clock curfew, you didn't expect him to walk you to the door and he didn't. It wouldn't have looked cool in front of his friend, you told yourself. So you opened your backseat door and threw an "OK, so I'll talk to you later," towards the Crown Vic as you walked towards your house, your familiar house. You wanted to call your best friend to debrief, but you knew she was probably with her sulky boyfriend, so you decompressed by yourself, avoiding your mom's questions about what you did: you didn't want to tell anyone you'd cruised the 'Bash, much less your MOM, who would be all "So what does that MEAN?"

Art called you a couple of days later and he was flirting, mentioning your black tank top and how you blended in with his car. You were sufficiently flattered to agree to hang out on Friday night again, and you ran outside when you saw his car pull into your driveway. You didn't want him to accidentally mention to your mom where you'd gone the last Friday.

His nondescript friend was in the car again, and you headed back towards his neighborhood to pick up another couple of friends. You stopped in a skankier neighborhood on the other side of 7th Street, and this WT girl in cheap short shorts and two WT guys in baggy t-shirts and baggy jeans squished in the backseat with you. You all said a curt, "Hey" to each other — no introductions. WT Guy #1, who was pushed against the other car window with the chick on his lap, leaned his arm out the window as Art rounded a corner slowly. "That fucking dog," WT Guy #1 muttered as WT Guy #2 asked, bored, "Did you get him?" "Fuck, no," said WT Guy #1, and your chest thudded for a second as you realized WT Guy #1 was holding a fucking HANDGUN, and he had been planning to SHOOT AT A DOG.

Everyone in the car seemed to be utterly nonplussed by the situation, but your mind was screaming I AM IN A CAR WITH A GUY WHO HAS A GUN! A GUN! HE JUST PULLED OUT A FUCKING GUN!

Art drove through town to a skanky "fun-plex" behind the mall, and you were secretly hoping Art was just giving WT Guys #1 and #2 and their Short Shorts chick a ride, that you'd leave them there. But Art turned off the engine and you all got out of the car, went inside and watched the WT boys play basketball. You couldn't believe you were in that corny place you'd dissed with your friends for the last few years as WHITE TRASH HEAVEN. You hoped at least Art would win some tickets at Skee-Ball and pick out a prize for you at the ticket counter, but he gave the tickets to some zombie-eyed middle-school boy playing Mortal Kombat.

WT Guy #2 mentioned a party some nameless WT girl was having at her house, and you all piled back in the car and drove to a neighborhood out by the federal penitentiary in your town. Art stopped in front of an ill-kempt house with one of those black lawn jockey statues by the front porch. You walked into this lame scene with three skanky WT girls holding cans of Bud Light and lounging on cheap dirty couches with two skanky WT guys sitting in front of a TV playing a video game. This was the first NO-PARENTS "party" you'd ever been to and it was the most depressing thing you'd ever seen. THIS was what people defied parental rules for? To drink grody beer and watch boys play VIDEO GAMES?

You didn't have anything to say to the girls and they didn't even try to say anything to you, but one of them recognized Art and started talking to him. You hung out near the hall, excused yourself to go to the bathroom just to have something to do, and when you came back, you watched the TV screen intently, like you cared, like you were REALLY INTO whatever stupid faux-Warcraft game they were playing. Your head was spinning and you were grateful no one was paying attention to you, even Art. You didn't know how you'd wound up out by the Pen with a bunch of WT drinking beer. You thought wildly about how your mom had always told you that, "no matter what," if you found yourself in a situation that made you uncomfortable, you could call her and she would come pick you up, no questions asked. But the prospect of asking one of the WT girls if you could USE THEIR PHONE and, particularly, the nightmarish fear of everyone in the house listening to you CALL YOUR MOMMY AND ASK HER TO COME GET YOU pushed that escape from your mind.

Besides, how could you explain to your mom what you yourself didn't understand: how you'd gone from flirting with this guy who looked like Art Alexakis at Summer Honors camp to being dragged into your town's seedy underworld of white trash lameness? How could you explain to your mom that being submerged in WT didn't bother you nearly as much as never being asked to sit in the front seat of Art's car?

Luckily, Art seemed to notice that it was almost your curfew and told one of the skanks that he'd be back later. To your chagrin, the WT Guys and Short Shorts decided to leave too, along with Art's friend, so you all piled back in the car and Art started winding down the back roads towards your neighborhood. WT Guy #1 hauled out his gun again and started shooting blindly into the corn fields, the report echoing through the dark night. HE JUST SHOT A FUCKING GUN. I AM IN A CAR WITH A GUY WHO JUST SHOT A FUCKING GUN, you thought to yourself, disbelieving you were where you were.

You got out of the car and tried to act nonchalant as you walked back into your house, knowing all the WT were watching. As you laid in your bed that night, you kept trying to piece the whole night together, convincing yourself alternately that WT Guy #1 DID have a gun, and also that he had been PRETENDING to have a gun. But the shots echoed through your memory, shot out through the drying cornstalks.

It took you four days to call Art Alexakis. He didn't answer when you called; his Homecoming Queen sister took your message. After a week had passed and he hadn't called you back, you washed your hands of the whole situation. You didn't really need to call him again for another night in White Trash Hell.

Your senior year of high school began a week or so later, and he wasn't in any of your classes, like you knew he wouldn't be. But you and Art would catch each other's eye in the hallway from time to time; neither of you would nod, or smile, but you'd lock eyes, acknowledging that you had known each other. Maybe Art thought he'd dragged you too far from your comfort zone once the gun had come out. But the thing was that he HADN'T. He had been there for the handful of weeks when you'd shed your skin, slipped into a girl so far from her honors-class behavior she was unrecognizable, a girl who could sit in a car with a boy shooting a gun, a girl who could sit on the curb on the 'Bash on a Friday night.

And that girl had taken root; you chopped your hair off, had your mom give you a haircut like the lead character in "Felicity," because your mom swore that your hair, which was wavy, might curl up as tight as hers if it was cut shorter. It didn't; you looked like a boy getting ready to enter the Armed Forces, but you liked it because it was no-nonsense, no-fucking-around, you-thought-I-wasn't-worth-kissing-I'll-SHOW-you-not-worth-kissing.

And Art Alexakis couldn't recognize you by the back of your head any more. No one could.

Maia Evrona

Hook

My older brother became ill suddenly when he was eleven, as if a bomb had exploded inside his nervous system. There were warnings before the explosion: they came while he was away at summer camp in Vermont. He had to spend a few days in the nurse's building, twice, sick with high fevers, headaches, and sore throats. The nurse assumed he had a simple summer bug he couldn't kick. My parents talked to each other about these episodes over dinner. Sitting with my legs crossed, Indian-style, in my seat at the table, I imagined the nurse's building at the summer camp: walls painted white, a nurse in a starched, white uniform, and Eli lying on the bottom of a bunk bed (I imagined that even the nurse's building had bunk beds), laughing and pulling pranks on the kids around him, as he always did. In the nurse's building of my mind, Eli winked at me like the joker of a deck of cards: colorful against a frame of white.

I learned later that there had only been one other boy in the nurse's building with Eli, and the boy had been there for a shorter period of time. The idea of my brother staying alone in the nurse's building stuck in my mind for months afterward. My parents brought him home sick again, with a fever, sore throat, and glands swollen-up like ping-pong balls. I went into the playroom to say hello, curious as to how he might have changed during our weeks apart, curious about the summer camp, and excited to tell him about my ninth birthday party. He greeted me with stories that we laughed over. But when we took a cruise to Bermuda soon after, Eli stayed in the cabin for most of the trip, seasick. On the whale-watches and deep-sea fishing trips we had taken summers before, Eli had never so much as gotten queasy. I spent my time with my five year-old brother Isaac at my left side. All the while I was aware of a void on my right: no one tickling me and teasing me, no one for me to protect Jake from, no one for Isaac to protect me from. Eli wasn't at summer camp anymore; his strange absence made me hold Isaac's hand tighter, and he was always squirming to get away from me, smothered.

Eli started middle school after our trip. He was tall and thin, with dark brown hair, brown eyes and high cheekbones: he came home with stories of all the girls who liked him. He told me how, in middle school, nobody brought their lunch, because there were so many more choices in the cafeteria, and a lunch box wasn't cool. I devoured his stories with my active, bookworm's imagination: Middle school! More friends to meet in a bigger building! The start of romance! Not to mention being the gateway to high school, which held even more excitement. He tried out for the town's travel soccer team as he did every year and, as every year, he was accepted. Of the three of us, he was best at sports. Because of Eli, I tried to play soccer, too, though I was small and frail, prone to getting sick. But that autumn, Eli twisted his knee and it took such a long time to heal that he spent the rest of the soccer season cheering his team on as he supported himself with crutches.

Eli began staying home from school sick more often, though he didn't always have a cold or the flu, just fevers. I listened, uneasily, to his happy stories of the first middle-school dance; I met the friends who slept over after. But not only did Eli not go back to school and see those friends after that, I hardly saw him myself: he spent his time in his room and then in the playroom running daily fevers of one hundred and four degrees, which were eventually accompanied by a migraine that didn't ease for two weeks. My parents took him to a doctor who diagnosed him with a migraine (it was already obvious that a migraine was what he had) but didn't bother trying to discover what could be causing it, nor give him anything for the pain. Instead, she prescribed cognitive-behavioral therapy. The migraines continued; as my mother drove me to school, she would tell me that Eli always had to keep the windows rolled down when she took him to appointments at Boston's Children's Hospital and Tufts, so he could vomit out the window. I listened often to the story of the neurologist who skimmed the chart my mother kept of Eli's fevers, looked at my mother and asked her why she was so fixated on her son's temperature. "What do you do when your son says he feels sick, shivers and looks flushed? You take his temperature!" she would repeat, furiously, to my father, to Eli's tutor, to my aunt over the phone.

Tension grew up the inside of our house like a vine: up the walls of the living room, covering the windows, curling around the banisters of the stairs, strangling the water faucets at the sink and choking the drains. The few times she drove me to school were the few times I saw my mother, for she was taking Eli to many doctors, and more and more preoccupied with catching up on the work she was missing. When she was at home, she was absorbed in finding responses to the doctors who accused Eli of school-phobia and bulimia and said he was just depressed because my grandmother had died the year before. She was rightfully furious with the teachers and school officials who still held Eli to the same due dates and busywork they assigned to healthy students.

Since my grandmother died, I had been plagued by fear that my mother was going to die as well. I thought it would happen sometime when I wasn't around and so, the anxiety grew worse as I saw her less, extending to my father and my brothers, though I never approached thinking that Eli could be dying of whatever was happening to him. I did know, listening to my mother's frenzied talk about how thin he was from my room upstairs, that it was time to start keeping my anxiety to myself. Often in the evenings, she and my father fought: my mother thought my father couldn't acknowledge how sick Eli was and was leaving his medical care up to her. On such nights, I would sit on the stairs, compelled to listen, until my father walked down the hall to their room and slammed the door, and I scurried back to mine. That year, my father began assistant coaching my soccer team, and I spent more time with him than ever. On the way to practice, I'd hold in the anxiety I felt, which was so intense it made me queasy, that now that I wasn't there our house was going to burn down, and I tried to ignore my father's irritation over how late we always were. Eventually, all other worries faded as my dread of soccer took over: I hated how painful running was, both on my joints and on my lungs, which didn't seem to bother anyone else. From time to time, my father mentioned that he had never gotten a chance to coach Eli's teams, and so, I would do my best to hide my tears as my breath slashed up my throat like a knife and my ankles smarted after half a lap around the soccer field.

Every memory I have from this time of Eli is dark, as if he had turned into an angry ghost who was haunting us. At night, I could feel him in my bedroom as I tried to fall asleep, facing the wall through which I listened to my parents taking care of his fevers and headaches. As I lay listening, tension snuck underneath my blanket and curled itself tightly around me. Sometimes I fell asleep, or woke up to the sound of Eli's restless legs pacing up and down the hallway that ran between his room and mine. Sometimes he fell asleep leaning against a wall, with his legs still kicking, like a somnambulant tap-dancer; his legs were always worst at night.

Tension completely filled what had formerly been the playroom, now transformed into Eli's sickroom. Isaac and I couldn't go in anymore. I remember daring to walk in only once that first winter he was sick. As soon as I opened the door, I was assaulted by the freezing air. Each time one of his fevers broke, like a wave coming to shore, Eli turned the air conditioning on. Sometimes I heard my father in there, yelling about the danger of the pipes freezing. The walls of the playroom were painted white, like the nurse's building I had imagined at the summer camp, but I could no longer imagine Eli as the colorful joker inside it. Instead, I found him lying on the couch, the migraine and fever squeezing his sunken, grimacing face from the inside. I muttered something about him always being in there using the television, never giving anyone else a turn. "Get the fuck out of here!" he shouted at me. He looked as if he was going to cry from the effort. A flaming arrow of shame shot down in front of me, red as a stop sign. I left immediately; the room was Eli's.

Lightheaded. My mother used the word all the time. She told me that he couldn't sit straight up: whenever she took him anywhere, he had to lean the front car seat all the way back. I didn't know what lightheaded meant.

Sometimes my mother talked about Eli blacking out, but I didn't connect it with the word lightheaded. I woke up one night to the sound of a steady banging, as if someone was slamming a book against a wall. The banging stopped suddenly, though I thought I heard a softer thud. I lay in bed awake, wondering if I had really heard anything at all. A gnawing sensation kept me from sinking back into sleep: I was strongly aware, perhaps because I wasn't sure that *I* had even heard it, that I was the one who had to see what, if anything, had made the noise. I wasn't scared. Sometimes, when just awakened, strange things seem to be of the expected. I learned this having a prankster for an older brother, who used to wake me at night by crawling under my bed and then beating against it from underneath, like a monster.

My room was next to the wide staircase that led down to our front door. I walked out into the hall, looked around, and then walked slowly down the stairs, careful because the lights above them were off. I didn't like turning on lights at night because it took my eyes a painfully long time to adjust from the dark to the light. So I didn't realize until I was almost at the bottom step that Eli lay on the raised landing at the bottom of the stairs. He was slumped onto his right side, with his back to the banisters lining the landing, his long, thin body wrapped in the shadow that collected there in the night. The banisters had broken his fall, stopped him from making one last three-foot drop into the entrance way below. By each side of the landing, there were two short sets of stairs. Eli's head and neck were on a slant, hanging into the steep drop down to the first step of the left set of stairs. My drowsy impression was that he looked out of place, lying on the landing as if it were a bed, with the thin, white banisters rising up behind him like an instrument of torture or the railings lining a ship in the dark. Once I knelt down next to him, I saw that his eyes were closed. Eli always seemed to me to sleep with a smile on his face, so I thought that he was faking, toying with me again.

"Eli, wake up," I whined, sleepy, annoyed, and cold in my thin nightshirt and socks. He didn't. "Eli, come on, wake up."

As I reached out to nudge him, I realized, with rising, nauseous dread, how afraid I was of touching him. *What if he isn't joking?* The thought woke me fully. *Why would he be doing this to me: faking sleep at the bottom of the staircase at 2 AM? How would he even know that I would hear him?* I realized that that the banging that had woken me had been his long legs smacking against the wooden banisters as he rolled down the stairs. I inched back from my brother's face, my own legs straightened, and, careful to avoid Eli's feet, I walked down the last few steps and then through the marble hallway to my parents' room. I knocked gently on the door, as I always did when I was little and had had a nightmare and didn't want to go back to sleep by myself, or had vomited during the night.

"Mom, Dad?" I called with my soft, nine-year old girl's voice, into the deep, dark space between their door and their bed.

"What?" one of my parents sleepily replied.

"Eli's lying at the bottom of the stairs and won't wake up."

"What!" my mother cried out of sleep.

"I think Eli fell down the stairs. He won't wake up."

My mother jumped up first. Then my father rolled out of bed, put his old kimono on over his white underwear, and came too. Back in the foyer, my father took Eli from the landing and lay him on the floor. My mother wanted to call an ambulance, but my father, who was a doctor, got Eli awake and moving himself, saying that an ambulance wasn't necessary. My mother tried, once more, to insist, as she knelt down and cradled Eli's head in her hands. She began talking to him and I heard him mumbling replies. I stood off by the side, feeling remarkably small, watching.

Matthew Muilenburg

The Belly Ache

I am a pornographer, a dealer of indecency. I'm the condom wrapper your ex-wife found under the bed, but didn't confront you about until you forgot to pick up three pounds of English cucumbers at the farmer's market on Sunday. I'm the dark, greasy building back behind the truck stop lit by a single, shy red bulb.

I'm the shame.

I'm the blame.

I'm a bad mammajamma, monsieur.

I was told all that, more or less, one cold afternoon by a tiny Thumbelina grandmother who had requested to speak to the editor of the newspaper. As I forced myself from my office and peaked around the corner to see who was requesting my attention, I immediately felt guilty for knowing that I wouldn't be apologizing that morning.

Barely five feet tall and shaped like a never-been-sucked candy cane — like her head was more susceptible to gravity than the rest of her body — the little old lady had come in to complain. She was ensconced in wrinkles, her hair too black for a woman in her eighties. Squinting through thick, smudged bifocals, she wore a lusterless gold crucifix around her neck. A sad cocktail of moles and liver spots chased a river of purple varicose up and down her thin arms, and the woman's white pantyhose, frayed around the ankles, appeared to have been bought with a buy-one-get-one-free Sears-Roebuck coupon that expired in 1955.

"What can I do for you?" I asked cautiously.

The woman stepped back like I was going to stomp her but quickly gathered herself. She spoke softly, but pointedly. "I just came in here to say that I am disgusted with what you did," she said, unable to look me in the eyes. "That picture you have on the front page — it's filth."

A few days earlier, I'd made the editorial decision to put the picture of a pregnant nineteen-year-old on the front page of that week's issue. The mother stood sideways, holding up her shirt, her nude, stretch-marked stomach popping out like a question mark. The story accompanying the photo was a downer: the fetus, a girl, had a disorder that was slowly pushing her heart to the right side of her body. Her intestines had begun to crawl up into her chest through a hole in her diaphragm and her tiny body bloomed just one full lung. There was a serious chance the baby wouldn't survive. Understandably, the overwhelmed mother sobbed several times as I interviewed her. She knew her daughter would never play sports or participate in P.E., but had hopes that the girl would become an artist one day. The story I wrote was sad. Moving. Heartbreaking.

Pornographic, too, apparently.

"I never thought this paper would publish something like that," the grandmother said, pointing at the front page of the paper sitting on a rack next to the secretary's desk. She looked away in revulsion, informing me that she'd come straight to the office from her weekly get-together of mothers. "We mothers are disgusted," she continued. "I thought you would be a better role model for our kids. I was going to write a letter to the editor about what you did, but what's the point?"

The point is that the little old lady had an opinion but refused to let it leave the rumor mill. In small towns like the one that paper served, neighbors won't offend anyone in print, but have few qualms about pushing thick waves of half-truths through that rumor mill. I discovered this long before the little old lady stormed our office. Within weeks of arriving in the community, I'd learned all about the raunchy affairs that had leapt from the groins of bored married men and women, and the children who congealed from the consummations. I learned who was a racist, who was a pretend Catholic, and who was thought to be a homosexual posing as a breeder. Which was the good priest and which was the bad. I learned who liked liquor and marijuana too much and who was pretending to be a virgin. I was even spun a detailed story about the dirty side of an economically important person in the community. Rumor had it that, years earlier, she let a married man slide off her panties behind the building where they were attendees of an annual fundraising gala. "She took it from behind," my source said, then proceeded to inform me that the woman was actually a transplant into the community, moving there a little less than a decade earlier. Like myself, she wasn't "of" that town; I always wondered if I would have been told that story if she was born and bred amongst the rumor mill.

That manner of discussion, that passive-aggressive verbal dialogue, was acceptable to people like the little old lady because it stayed in the whispers. Talk about it all you want, just don't write about it.

"Well, we'd be happy to publish a letter if you change your mind," I told the little old lady, needling her, knowing she would never print her opinion.

"Well, what's the point?" she repeated. "It wouldn't make any bit of difference."

"I'm sorry to hear that," I said. "If you change your mind, we'll be here."

The little old lady looked at me through those blurry bifocals with eyes much sadder than the scowl she featured below. She ached for an apology, her sense of ethical superiority needing to suckle on my confession of guilt. To her, I was a spoiled brat who dunked her rosary in tainted holy water, and she yearned to hear me say I was sorry. A face-to-face apology, however, would not be enough. She wanted to see our paper genuflect to her moral authority in print, needing to run her wrinkled fingertips over one word — Sorry — in the next edition.

Once she knew there would be no apology, the little old lady trudged out of the office, sighing and waving off my final attempt to get her to write in. I stared out of the door for a few minutes after she left, trying to gather myself. I couldn't believe what I just heard, unable to understand how one of the most revered sights throughout history, a pregnant woman's stomach, had just been equated to a Jenna Jameson spread.

The solicitous eyes and ears dawdling about the newsroom during the encounter flipped from my line of sight as I turned around and stomped into the editorial room, slamming the door and bellowing "What the fuck is going on here?!" The little old lady's visit was my last straw, the finale in a stream of one-sided conversations I had with readers livid over the stomach. I was told I had no morals, that readers thought my paper was repulsive, that I was ruining young minds and publishing Playboy. Coffee klatches chaired by *Leave it to Beaver* Bettys exploded in fraught. All of them: fed up, outraged. Queasy even. Some shouted. Some gritted their teeth. Sometimes their voices shook as they held back tears (over a belly). One reader said he could see the girl's panties, mistaking the pink camouflage waistband of her black, stretchy maternity pants for underwear. Before we printed, my publisher warned me that we'd get backlash from the community for forcing upon their virgin eyes such quantities of flesh, but I refused to believe her.

"It's just a stomach," I said.

"Not to some people," my boss said.

Ah, yes. *Some* people: the Norman and Norma Rockwells in the community, the Two Straw and One Milkshake Gang who used to ask for cherries on top in the '50s before becoming, sixty years later, the black coffee ombudsmen and decaf first ladies who occupy the back ends of fast food restaurants each morning. They'd come from farming families, and from value sets with rules rigidly resistant to progressive swings in the community, state, and country. These people held sway socially, sometimes politically. One of the town's city council members claimed to be a staunch liberal, yet did everything in her power to keep the community from changing, from growing. She voted against an economic development that would have drawn in thousands of people each summer and brought millions in tax revenue. She was irrational and fond of speaking from both sides of her mouth. But she was also "of" the town. The Milkshakers adored her.

These people were upset because I inadvertently brought them an outside world they wanted to still be in chastity belts, dragged in what they only saw on magazines in the supermarket: skin, a whole belly's full of it. I splashed it on the front page of their hometown paper, made them confront what they wanted to deny: the unwed are procreating. For that, I became Larry

Flint's Midwest cohort, John Holmes' wordsmithing doppelganger, Hugh Hefner's heir to the throne of immorality.

And I'm fine with that.

I'm not fine, however, when you put the story into context. In the months leading up to that picture, we didn't receive one single complaint about the material we printed on the front of the paper. We told the story of a man who blasted his wife in the head with a shotgun and described how another man beat his estranged girlfriend bloody while their preteen daughter watched. We published stories on meth lab busts and on a father who took his three-year-old daughter on a joy ride on his motorcycle. In the middle of winter. Without a helmet. We wrote a story about the extortion attempt of a multimillion dollar company new to the area and another about a man who threatened to hew his stepfather in half with a samurai sword. We wrote about a former troop mom who bilked thousands from the Girl Scouts for her own use. We put a story about the local superintendent, who drank himself into a DUI, across the top of page one. And yet, despite all of this, I never received a phone call or an email or a letter to the editor, not even a dirty look or a drop of poison in my milkshakes, over my decision to slap most of the bad news on the front page. None of that shook these people's centers, made them question our values, forced them to come into our office to chew on me like a ball gag.

We didn't shoot anyone in the head, sell them meth, or beat them savagely in front of their daughters. On the night that girl sobbed at the sight of her father bludgeoning her mother, we reported that the victim bolted out of the apartment when the cops arrived, her face drenched in blood. She screamed for help.

And our readers screamed for more.

I recently began watching American Horror Story, an hour-long cable show. As the title suggests, there is an executioner's manifesto of sadism and horror that is asphyxiated into one hour of viewing each week. In one episode, a young virgin is stabbed in the back over and over as she strains against the binds that keep her hands and feet lassoed behind her back. Another woman is shot through the eye with a handgun. A teen channels Columbine and murders fifteen teenagers with his shotgun (earlier in the day, he poured gasoline on his stepfather and lit a match). A twenty-something male is gutted with an axe, and a young, pregnant college student is bludgeoned to death with a shovel. An abortion doctor sews dismembered babies back together. There's death by fire, death by drowning, death by suicide.

All of that explicit murdering made me squirm, but I didn't verbalize my uneasiness until the female protagonist fails to achieve orgasm. In that scene, our heroine tries desperately to bring herself to climax by fantasizing about the glorified security guard who watches over her house. In the middle of this fantasy, frightening images penetrate her mind and she loses all her momentum. That's when she sits up in bed, fully dressed. We don't see her nipples, pubic hair, or buttocks. We don't even see her stomach. We simply see her rise, breath heavily, and turn off a vibrator. And that's when I gasped. After all that blood, all that death, all that sadism, I didn't react negatively until a vibrator appeared on screen.

I realized then that the conditioning worked, that no matter how ridiculous I find the argument that an exposed belly is offensive and that violence isn't, there is part of me, the shyest, least confident part, that agrees. I'm part of the group that makes violent stories the top read on most news sites. I'm the one who used to gobble down the police reports before putting them into the paper. I'm the consumer who rents Jason, Hannibal, Freddy, Michael, and Jigsaw for ninety minutes at a time. I'm also the one who is shocked to see a vibrator.

Maybe I'm a traitor to my own value set. Or maybe I reacted that way because I don't see many rumbly-tumbly phallic devices on TV or in print. There's not enough space or time for them with all the rape and murder.

A couple weeks after we printed the belly, as the office eased back to normality, I made another decision that I knew would cause a rift. Twice each year, we printed a magazine that highlighted area families with a story to tell. As we outlined the spring issue, I suggested we write about a family whose matriarch was a professional bodybuilder and personal trainer (I'd heard about her through the rumor mill). Months earlier, when I was out on assignment, she held a photo shoot across the street from the office, wearing a few threads of clothing and rubbing her muscles up and down a shiny motorcycle. People whispered about that for months. My coworkers, male and female, old and young, most of them "of" the community, practically exploded when they told me about it upon my return.

I took on the story. After interviewing the bodybuilder and her family, I asked the mother if she could provide some photos from her competition, particularly one of her and her husband and kids after the contest was over. She said she'd try to find one, but a few days later I received something wholly different: a picture of the mother in her thong bikini, flaunting her physique on stage: hard breasts sculpted beneath the shiny triangles of a pink bikini top; oiled, glistening muscles spilling from her arms; long legs waxed and shiny and leading up to the buffed chalice from which her children were poured seventeen years earlier. Her stomach was also bare. Rippling, toned. Without child.

When I decided to run that picture on the front cover (juxtaposed next to a traditional family shot that was intended to show the mother's duality), I prepared myself for warfare. I went down into the doomsday bunker, rallied the scantily clad troops, and got all my sticks and stones in a row.

The next morning, I woke with a stomach ache that lingered like morning sickness. I was confident that my decision to put that picture on the cover was the right one, artistically-speaking; I also told myself that I wasn't abusing my power and printing the photo out of spite. After our editorial meeting ended around noon that day, five hours after many in the community would have gotten their papers, I stepped cautiously into my office and saw the red voicemail light blinking. I sighed and rubbed my face and plopped down in my chair. I punched in the code on the phone and opened my email as I waited for the voicemail to play. Expecting to be bombarded with the same types of messages that flooded my inbox the day we published the belly, I was overwhelmed with blessed confusion to see that no one had written in to complain. Not one word eschewing our lost virtues. Not one tear shed for the community's loss of innocence. Not one offended reader.

The voicemail kicked in then, and I listened to a local government official tell me that we shouldn't be putting such profane garbage on the cover of our publications. I hit delete when he said, "A return phone call won't be necessary; the damage has been done." The robot voice informed me then, to my surprise, that I was out of messages.

I sat back in my chair, shaking my head, relieved yet agitated. I wanted confrontation. Needed it. I'd prepared for it, acknowledged it, welcomed it. There were buttoned-up and long-skirted demons I needed to exercise. Smudged bifocals I wanted to clean. Lusterless crucifixes I wanted to polish. Ratty pantyhose I wanted to swap out for a modern pair.

But I never got the chance.

No one else called in that day to complain about our pornography. They didn't call the next day, the next week, or the next month either. And even though I was told by some in the community that people were still judging us, it wasn't enough. I wanted to hear all of this firsthand, wanted to use my sticks and my stones, wanted someone else to come in and challenge my moral center.

But this time, I only got to hear about it through the rumor mill.

Robert F. Sommer
Remedial Army

"For death has made me wise and bitter and strong;
And I am rich in all that I have lost."
– Siegfried Sassoon

We have eleven hand-written letters from Francis during Basic Training at Fort Benning, more than he wrote in the next five years of active duty, including his tours in Iraq and Afghanistan. We packed him off with a stack of pre-addressed, stamped envelopes and a pad of plain paper. We were so new to this we didn't know postage was free. All of his letters arrived on that stationary.

The requirements for writing to him were very particular: block print and black ink on white envelopes. No packages. Nothing in the envelope but a letter, photos, clippings, phone cards. One recruit did 200 pushups when a letter arrived in a yellow envelope. Another made a wisecrack about a flowery card Francis got from his mother.

"My mother sends me cards," the drill sergeant snapped, "so shut the fuck up!"

Years later we found that card among his things, folded and creased, as worn out as a garage rag. It had traveled many miles tucked in his pocket or helmet.

In his fine book, *Epistolary Practices: Letter Writing in America before Telecommunications,* William Merrill Decker describes a letter as existing in a "continuous present tense." So it is with these letters from Francis, all written with a ballpoint pen on lined sheets of notepaper. The pages have texture. They crackle and flutter. You hold them rather than look at a back-lit screen. Only one original exists, dated, signed, folded, slipped into an envelope, sealed on the tip of his tongue. The depression of the pen on the page, the curl of his handwriting — these are traces of him in motion, active, alive. Each one a creation of hand and body, of language and spirit.

A continuous presence.

✦

He was a good writer, if not a good student.

Graduated from high school, just. College, not on the horizon. But with an IQ in the mid-140s, his aptitudes were high. I have a fixed memory of the sharp breath a school counselor drew when he reviewed Francis's first grade test results with us. He said he'd never seen verbal scores like this. Nothing about his comment suggested hyperbole or flattery. He seemed genuinely wide-eyed. Francis had exceptional ability. He learned quickly, remembered things easily, and as he grew, questioned everything from TV commercials to politics, usually in ways that accentuated their absurdity. He had a quick wit and was very funny, though his sarcasm could be acidic (though still very funny). We read to him from an early age, especially Heather. He loved books and reading and being read to. He spent much of a long car ride to Colorado when he was eleven or so buried in *D'Aulaires' Book of Greek Myths*. (We also had to backtrack thirty or forty miles on that trip so he could return the trinkets he pocketed in a souvenir shop and offer a sullen apology to the owner as I stood by.)

But as a student he was impatient, easily distracted, impish. Years later, after he enlisted and deployed overseas, his grade school principal and I laughed about the time he got caught in fifth grade with a pocketful of condoms. Wasn't so funny when I had to drop everything at work to go deal with it. How he got them, who knew? But at fifty-cents apiece there seemed to be a profitable market among ten-year-old boys with more ambition than prospects (or need).

But he wrote well — in confident sentences and a clear and personable voice.

"Hi everybody!" he greeted us. Or "Hello family!" Or "Hi Sommers!"

His new first name, we learned, was "You."

His letters are observant. They tell us about the people he's meeting, narrate his new life:

> Then on Tuesday... the gas chamber!! Everybody was really pumped to go through the CS[1] chamber, but attitudes were different on the inside. I hated it. How terrible! At first with the gas mask on, I didn't think it was that bad, just a little burning on the neck and hands, and watery eyes. But with the mask off, I couldn't even open my eyes and all I could do was cough. Then someone dropped their weapon, so we got to do pushups. ☹ Like I said, I hated it.

The passage goes on to describe chemical warfare, the higher grade of gas they may face in battle, the Geneva Convention's proscriptions against such weapons.

A few days later, the recruits are getting ready for "our first real road march with our rucksacks (with 30 pound loads and bedrolls), equipment belts, weapons, and Kevlar helmets."

He continues:

> I'm not sure how long it is, but I'm sure we'll be beat when we're done. By the end of training, we will have completed a 25-mile road march in all that equipment with the exception that there will be about 70 – 80 lbs. in our rucks (camping equipment, etc.). I have heard some guys in the church that are later in the cycle requesting personal prayers that they

---

1   So-called for Ben Corson and Roger Stoughton, who invented this form of tear gas.

and their platoon will make it through that particular march.

The hard part, we learn, isn't the weight of the pack: "…what's difficult is carrying your weapon at the 'ready' position. Especially in the early morning heat when the sweat combines with the moisture in the air and makes it really slippery."

This was Georgia in mid-June. A few weeks later they found themselves clearing rattlesnakes from the sand pits in which they'd sleep (or lie awake all night as fits of rattling in the field startled them into vigilance) and checking boots and sleeping bags before putting feet or bodies in either.

He was meeting people from all over the country and around the world: "In my platoon there is a kid from Russia who's been here for 2 years. There's also a guy from the Caribbean and one from Mexico." But most compelling for their stories and talk are the New Yorkers:

> At the Reception Battalion, I was right in the mix with a lot of New Yorkers — mostly Puerto Ricans and from all five boroughs. I like listening to them talk — they have their own dialect going on. ("My dome looks mad crazy without no hair, yo." ☺

He profiled the drill sergeants for us, too:

> The DS's for my platoon are probably about 26 and about 40. The older one is actually the cooler one. He motivates us a lot and likes to hang out in the barracks and answer our questions about Army life and tell stories. He served in Desert Storm with the 101st Airborne Division. The younger one is going to Ranger school this fall. All the DS's are either E6 or E7 — Staff Sergeant or Sergeant First Class.

Such details were not wasted on us. We were in remedial-Army, learning ranks, pay grades, what the different divisions did, where they were based — what a division was.

On a quiet Sunday in early July, he wrote to us about a pro football player who would start training the next day:

> Apparently he is (was) a safety for the Cardinals and turned down a big contract to train as an Airborne Ranger instead. I don't know the guy personally but if he's at reception right now, he may be regretting his decision a little. I think his biggest challenge will be keeping his cool around a bunch of guys who don't understand about discipline and doing the right thing and who weren't taking it seriously. I know I was surprised by some of the people here and how incompetent they are. As I write this in the afternoon, there are guys lying around sleeping when we were told all we had to do today after cleaning was stay awake.

A couple had gone AWOL too, which the older DS shrugged off, saying he was surprised it took so long. Happened in every group, the DS said. More notable than a high-profile athlete in camp was our son lecturing us on "discipline and doing the right thing and…taking it seriously." This was headline news to us.

Pat Tillman was the public face of waves of enlistees who joined in response to the 9/11 attacks. At eighteen Francis breathed the same air we all shared in the months that followed. He'd caught the fever of patriotism. Images of first-responders in uniforms had filled TV screens for months. An intense atmosphere of tragedy settled like thick fog over America — which now became the *homeland*. A toxic desire for revenge had juiced homeland America in 2002, when Francis enlisted. Just two years later, a Marine in Iskandariah, Iraq, where Francis was also deployed at the time, spoke for a generation of recruits when he told a *Washington Post* reporter why he enlisted: "To be honest, I just wanted to take revenge." A stiff cocktail of patriotism and vengeance had galvanized many, like this young man and Francis, with a sense of purpose. Yet now that Marine could find no connection between the events of 9/11 and the invasion of Iraq. "Sometimes I see no reason why we're here," he said.[2]

9/11, Francis wrote, was a frequent topic among recruits:

> It was also interesting to hear their different stories about where they were and what they were doing on the morning of Sept. 11. The one I remember most vividly is this kid telling me how he ran all the way from where he worked in Manhattan across the Queensborough Bridge to Bushwick in Brooklyn, and when he got to his apartment the phones were not working so he had to wait all day for his family to come home to see if they were okay.

The tone of his letters is mostly upbeat; they're written in good spirits. It's impossible to measure the gap between the reality of daily life in basic and the narrative he shared, but he was not given to hiding his moods. If things weren't going well, he wouldn't have written as often, if at all. And we'd have known it.

The year or two leading up to his enlistment had been a difficult time. Late one night when he was still in high school, a policeman appeared at the car window after Francis and the kid behind the wheel had just finished sharing a joint. That was all the dope they had on them, one roach in the ashtray. Like the condoms incident, even this seems like small change now, but it consumed us then. The drug possession charge landed us in court, followed by a diversion program and probation. One night out for two high school kids turned into a long and expensive year for all of us.

After graduation he was amazed at how quickly the next year passed. He got a job in a hardware store and moved into an apartment with a crew that fed on low expectations and lurched from one dreary party to the next. He told me later that he'd begun to fret about people he knew appearing at his cash register, about being seen there and having nothing but a shrug

---

2   Steve Fainaru, "For Marines, a Frustrating Fight: Some in Iraq Question How and
    Why War Is Being Waged," Washington Post, Sunday, October 10, 2004, Sect. A, p. 1.

to offer when someone asked what his plans were. He knew he was going under. America's entry into Afghanistan and the "war on terror" came at a moment when he needed a lifeline. The Army tossed him one — and us too, so it felt at the time. He came home one day with a stack of recruitment brochures and spread them out on the kitchen table.

His first phone call from Fort Benning came two days after we put him on the plane. He was so stressed, frantic even, that the call left us more worried than reassured. It lasted about sixty seconds. A required call home: *I'm here, I'm alive, the plane didn't crash, I didn't run off!* I took the call and heard loud, harsh voices echoing all around him and finally a sergeant telling him to wrap it up. Wasn't hard to picture the recruits lined up, waiting their turns for the phone, herded off to whatever was next — medical exams, shoe fittings, equipment checkout. In rookie military-parent time, sixty seconds on the phone equals a week of worry and doubt. We parsed every syllable, every echo, every anything we could wring out of that call. Had he done the right thing? Would he make it through the next sixteen weeks? He said we wouldn't hear from him again for a while.

So his letters, which began to arrive the following week, came as a welcome surprise and opened a window on a side of him we'd only glimpsed in recent times and a world about which we knew little. The writing was honest, we felt, and basic training maybe wasn't as awful as we imagined after that first call. We knew he'd survive. There was enough bluntness, and snark, in his letters to authenticate them. But now, reading through them again, I also notice how often the word *fun* appears: "The past three days have been the most fun I've had since I've been here ..." Then in the next letter, and without a hint of sarcasm, "This week should be fun." And later, ahead of a week-long camping exercise: "I think it will be fun, and even if it rains a lot, it'll be no sweat for me, right Dad? ☺" — referring to a soggy camping trip in the Rockies we'd taken a year or so earlier. He also mentions that he hadn't seen any women since he arrived. Not surprising, since infantry divisions are all-male and basic training units at Fort Benning are segregated in an area known as Sand Hill.

His sister Erin remarked that he only complained about one thing: complainers.

"Oh, well," he wrote, "imagine how it was 200 years ago. That's a little saying around here for every time someone complains."

That theme remained with him throughout his years in the Army and beyond, the perspective of history, how difficult life was for soldiers of earlier generations, how email, Skype, satellite phones, and Goretex had changed deployments. Soldiers in battle zones were sometimes distracted, he said, tracking money as it disappeared from bank accounts, arguing with spouses and girlfriends about routine problems at home, worrying about whether they were unfaithful, which happened to a few guys he knew. He worried about the danger such distractions might pose.

Years later he said boot camp was the easiest thing he ever did in the Army. He wrestled in high school, played football, and ran track. He was out of shape when he enlisted, but like many young recruits, his physical abilities hadn't faded altogether. Basic was extreme summer camp for big boys, for some anyway. It was misery for others, we also heard. The biggest thrill came when they began firing automatic weapons, blowing things up, simulating battles in laser-tag exercises, paintball *in extremis*.

With all the confidence of a novice and in chillingly detached prose, he instructs us in one letter on the proper technique for firing a rifle:

> The major trick is the trigger squeeze. If you squeeze to [sic] fast, your body naturally jerks in anticipation of the recoil. You have to go slow enough so that you don't know the exact moment of discharge....

None too comforting to parents, his new skill, his enthusiasm for firearms. The Fort Benning website has been overhauled since I combed it almost daily over a decade ago to follow his training. Now you can watch videos of recruits engaged in these activities. These boys do like the firing ranges, the soldiers on camera anyway, the ones you see, the ones you're supposed to see. Gaming is the dominant metaphor in all the interviews. Gaming on steroids. *Warcraft*-writ-large, *Assassin's Creed* ten-point-zero. Noise and action they couldn't dream up in their wildest, Red Bull-charged fantasies with a Play Station hitbox: three-dimensional imagery, monster woofers blowing back tidal waves of noise and heat from across an artillery range, the adrenaline rush of unleashing an M-249 Squad Automatic Weapon on a company of plywood bad guys.

Not likely that Heather and I are the target audience for these trailers.

No blood, of course, no severed limbs, no hemorrhaging arteries, no shrieking in agony; no quivering with life-and-death fear, no torn, lifeless bodies, enemy or friend, civilian or soldier, woman or child. War is still an abstraction, draped in the haze of billowing flags and melancholy renderings of "God Bless America"; entwined in the indistinguishable urgings of patriotism and vengeance — or, let's get real, the excuses they provide for big boys to play with expensive big-boy toys.

We were complicit. We shared his enthusiasm, or at least we were glad for his.

On our first visit to Fort Benning for Francis's mid-cycle pass, we stayed on post. We wanted to experience the Army up close. Heather and Erin and I went. His older brother Alex couldn't take time off from work.

There's a bitter and tragic irony in recalling our arrival. As we approached the front gate, we were confronted by the sight of a car so mangled into a clump of twisted metal and broken glass that at first glance it was unrecognizable for what it was. Where you'd expect to find a cannon or statue on this blanket of manicured grass, instead a horrifying wreck was displayed so no one coming or going through the gate would miss it — a cautionary emblem against drunk driving. Not on our expectation radar that day. We were amazed to think such incidents happened often enough to justify placing this wreck here. A message, we thought, for *other* soldiers, not ours. This could not happen to us. It would be nine years before I'd visit a salvage yard in Kansas to claim a wreck just like this one, have the title transferred to my name, and arrange for the car's disposal just days after we buried Francis. But a great deal lay ahead before that day would come.

Not far from our motel on post we strolled one evening on the quiet tree-lined lanes where officers and their families lived in white clapboard homes and sedate duplexes with toys scattered on thin lawns now parched by the long hot weeks of summertime in Georgia. Several scenes from the movie *We Were Soldiers* were filmed here, including the powerful sequence in which the colonel's wife takes over for a distraught mailman whose duty included delivering casualty notices to the wives who lived on these streets while their husbands were deployed in Vietnam.

He wore a short-sleeve dress shirt, pressed olive-green slacks, and a cadet cap. Our photos reveal his misgivings about being seen in this outfit, which he wore for the first time that day, a requirement of the weekend pass. His belt buckle is askew and his shirt partly untucked in one picture. The confidence he'd enjoyed for weeks on Sand Hill in workout gear or BDUs was now diluted by his first venture onto the main post in a blank uniform, devoid of color or rank — so obviously a trainee that he made an easy target even for a clerk in the commissary, who treated him with disdain and a clear sense of impunity about doing so as he got fitted for boots. (I was ready to give someone an earful about it too, but he said I'd only do more harm than good, and I'm sure he was right.) Later in town, he failed to salute an officer, who sent a double-whammy his way but let it pass. Francis was so nervous walking past the man that he became flummoxed. The officer had the good sense to know this wasn't worth trouble enough to humiliate him in front of his family.

We toured the post, visited the museum, ate Chinese food. What he most craved was sleep, and he did — through Friday evening, while we went to a baseball game. Columbus had a minor league team then, the Red Stixx, Cleveland's single-A farm club. Not much compares with minor-league baseball on an August night in a Southern town. We had great seats for a nominal price and brought home bobble-head dolls of the Goody-Goody Peanut Man, honored that night after thirty years of service at the ballpark. Heather's souvenir still stands in her classroom, an icon of good cheer and persistence to inspire her students.

Back at our room Francis slept on — right through until Saturday morning. We ate breakfast at the McDonald's on post, where he pointed out how many sergeants surrounded us, "the backbone of the Army," he said, intoning a phrase he'd picked up, proud of his own new standing. Rest and food had recharged him. The transformation was evident, from his posture and fitness to his attitude. *Transformation* isn't quite right. What these past twelve weeks had more accurately accomplished was distilling him, finding the essence beneath the encrusted layers of despair we'd seen and felt ourselves before he joined. Here he was isolated from TV, from booze and drugs; physically challenged to extremes a high school coach couldn't demand without risking a lawsuit; fed well, but not overfed; made to take care of personal hygiene and belongings and living space in ways a mother could only dream of. Yes, he was being indoctrinated too (though even that only served later to bring out his independent streak), but it was not possible right now to say that *this* wasn't better than *that,* that the place he'd been before wasn't worse than the place he'd now landed. And no one felt this more than him.

The recruits were required to check-in at the barracks mid-way through the weekend. One minute late and the pass would be cancelled. We'd come over nine hundred miles for this visit and weren't about to have him swiped away. We made it with time to spare, then watched as several families saw their soldiers rush into formation just that late and then disappear into the barracks for the rest of the weekend. Another lost his privilege because he was out of uniform. Friends, girlfriends, parents all muttered in disgust at the injustice of it, but everything conspired to change the behaviors not only of these young men, but, it would seem, anyone close to them. To round out the weekend, recruits were drug-tested on Sunday night. Francis stood in line until 2:00 AM waiting his turn.

Mid-cycle is a misnomer. We returned four weeks later for graduation. This time we stayed in town. Enough full-frontal Army. We didn't regret staying on-post for our first visit, but civilians are foreigners on an Army post. You need a military ID just to buy toothpaste.

Columbus is an Army town: fast food chains, tattoo shops, used car lots lined with rows of gleaming trucks and the promise of easy credit, dozens of quick-loan storefronts with barred windows. Still, my journal entries from that visit describe our pride and enthusiasm. We'd sipped the Kool-Aid. He'd done something special, proven things to himself, tested his limits and discovered they were farther than he imagined. He'd told Staff Sergeant Alexander, his recruiter, that he wanted to do the hardest things you could do in the Army. That moment at our kitchen table seemed like an age ago. He'd been assigned to the 10th Mountain Division. He would do hard things.

Heather pinned his infantry cord on him at the "turning blue" ceremony the day before graduation. The platoon commander warned fathers, don't even think about trying to match push-ups with your son. The ceremony the next morning was open-air theater staged on a wide tarmac parade ground with bleachers at one end and dense woods surrounding it. As the band played, columns of soldiers could be seen making their way through the pine trees to the far end of the field. Soon the show began: marching drills, tactical demonstrations (we learned the components of a squadron that day — our education in all-things-Army continued), a Bradley tank rumbling and spinning through its maneuvers, a loud and smoky finale with blank mortar rounds thundering as "Bad to the Bone" boomed across the field. We cheered our soldiers as mortar fusillades shook the bleachers.

But I also recall being overwhelmed by a sense of what this all meant, what deadly business we'd taken up here with these machines, this equipment, all this training and these men in uniforms. The cheers and whooping in the crowd seemed like a veneer that coated it. The passion of some in the bleachers was frightening — even more so than the machinery and guns. Perhaps we were just as frightening to others who felt similar doubts when they saw us smiling and applauding. We'd all been swept into the same current and could only swim downstream, some maybe swimming faster than others. Our strokes would be effortless if we didn't fight the current, even as familiar landscape along the banks disappeared and we were taken off to we-knew-not-where. Some on the field would not live through what came next. Towns and villages we didn't know existed and with names we couldn't pronounce would be turned to rubble. Tens of thousands of civilians in foreign countries would die, uncounted and nameless to us. Our casualties would be listed each week in newspapers, scrolled across TV screens with billowing flags behind the passing names, while those foreign casualties would remain clouded in numbers and submerged in page six stories — *"Fifty Iraqis Killed over the Weekend" "U.S. Airstrike at Taliban Kills Civilians, Afghans Say"* (so those Afghans say, so the newspaper says). Even then, in late 2002, fear and confusion and bitterness clouded our public discourse like the sulfurous smoke from these mortars. (Years later, after we'd lost Francis, Heather and I bristled at a Memorial Day service when a chaplain described how invigorating he found smoke from an honorary cannon fusillade, the literal fog of war.) More than a decade of war loomed beneath the horizon — and continues to this day — as we throbbed to *b-b-b-bad to the bone* on that overcast morning.

He wrote to us four years later from "some nameless mountain" in Afghanistan. The note was scrawled on thick brown card stock, the only one like it we ever received, preprinted on an MRE container soldiers could tear off to use as a postcard. "Sucks being the first guys here," he said. He filled both sides of the card describing the forward operating base they were building:

> We are the first U.S. forces to integrate a base camp with the Afghan Army. Needless to say, lots of top brass has been around lately, and reporters... [M]y platoon will be a part of history....

He also said he hadn't showered for a month and his beard was huge. He shared some details about his upcoming leave too, which he planned to take in Spain, where his sister was in school and we would meet him for a week. He was angry about being required to take his leave only four months into a planned twelve-month tour, which thanks to the new Stop-Loss policy, turned into sixteen months. Unknown to him or us, a full year in those mountains still lay ahead after his leave.

Tragic news awaited when he returned from Spain. While he was enjoying ten days on the sunny, semi-nude beaches of Barcelona, his unit had engaged in a fierce firefight and two of his friends were killed. He should have been with them, he thought. They needed him there.

That card was the last of his handwritten notes or letters in the Army. He scribbled all over the margins, trying to make the pen work on the thick card stock. A postscript declared, "MRE postcards suck."

He didn't like the food much either.

Francis's letter to his family, dated July 7, 2002, Fort Benning, GA.

7 JUL 02

Hi again. The weekend is finally coming to an end. No one around here is very fond of weekends because they go so slow and we have to clean a lot. But I like it sometimes because we can go to church and write letters and have some down time. We have had the last few days off from training, however, and everyone is ready to start back up again.

This week should be pretty challenging. We have a PT test tomorrow morning, and on Wednesday we have a 12-mile road march. We will also be training with hand grenades.

We heard that a proffessional football player starts training tomorrow. Apparently he is (was) a safety for the Cardinals and turned down a big contract to train as an Airborne Ranger instead. I don't know the guy personally but if he's at reception right now, he may be regretting his decision a little. I think his biggest challenge will be keeping his cool around a bunch of guys who

don't understand about discipline and
doing the right thing and who aren't taking
it seriously. I know that I was surprised
by some of the people here and how
incompetent they are. As I ~~write~~ write this in
the afternoon, there are guys lying around
sleeping. when we were told all we
had to do today after cleaning was stay
awake. ~~When~~ Oh well. Pretty soon we will
start to see people go home for various
reasons. I'm sort of glad, because I feel
like some people are dragging others
down. Two guys went A.W.O.L. yesterday
morning. It was surprising to us, but our
drill sergeant said he was surprised that
it took this long for someone to run off.

    Not much else going on. Could
you please send my Nike sports watch
if it is allowed by the post office? I
don't want to waste money on one
but I probably should have one. Also
some white boxer briefs would be handy.
Thanks a bunch. Well, bye for now. Love,
                Frank

Francis DiClemente

Man on the Stoop

On a sunny evening in early August last year, I walked along James Street in Syracuse, New York, trying to find a store where I could buy a bottle of water. I was in the Eastwood neighborhood to attend a poetry reading at Books & Melodies bookstore.

I passed a red brick building with a sign that read, "Furnished Efficiencies for Lease." A slim man in his late 50s or early 60s sat on the small stoop of the building, his head raised and his eyes focused on the traffic moving along James Street.

I continued striding down the block until I found The Burger Joint restaurant. I went in, grabbed a bottle of water from the cooler and paid for it at the counter. I then walked back to the bookstore, approaching the apartment building again.

I wanted to stop and talk to the man on the steps; something about his appearance made me wonder about his life. I wanted to learn more about him, to introduce myself and ask him some questions. As I came within a few feet of the building, he looked up at me, acknowledging my presence, and our eyes met. But I lost my nerve to greet him. I lacked the courage to open my mouth and say "hello," and the opportunity to interact with him and gain insight into his life was lost. I also regretted not having my camera with me because I think his strong profile would have made for a nice portrait.

He wore a dark T-shirt, jeans and sneakers, and his salt-and-pepper hair and thin mustache gave him a sort of rugged cowboy appearance. Wrinkles had worked their way into his careworn face, and he had a lean, hungry look, like he could have been the Marlboro Man a few decades earlier. He had oval eyes that were more vertical than horizontal. Mostly, though, he just looked tired, as if life had been dragging him down.

I will call him Sam because he reminded me of a Sam. Perhaps he was a factory
worker, a mechanic, a carpenter or a truck driver. I imagined if he spoke his voice would
sound something like actor Sam Elliott's.

And I pictured him in his small studio upstairs with its twin mattress, small desk and wooden chair, tiny bathroom and a window with broken

Venetian blinds.

I wondered how this man spent his days. Was he retired? Did he work? Was he an alcoholic or a drug addict? I also thought about the hot, humid night and how he needed to sit on the stoop to escape the stifling air in his apartment devoid of air conditioning.

Something in his body language reflected the universal struggle of human beings grappling with the challenges of each day, carrying around our flesh as we creep toward death. I felt pity for this man, and I am not sure why. He looked exhausted but not depressed, and he seemed content to stare out at the street and see the activity going on, to pass some time before darkness descended and he would retire for the night, trying to fall asleep in the sauna of his apartment.

But driving home after the poetry reading I thought to myself, "Who am I to assume what this man's life is like?" I only had his outward appearance to judge him by — and this was for just a few seconds as I walked to The Burger Joint for my water and headed back to the bookstore to attend the poetry reading.

What did I really know about this man?

Then again, what do we ever know by sight alone? I couldn't possibly understand the scope and scale and depth of this man's life based on a few cursory glances in his direction. I would have loved to sit with him on the steps, share a cup of coffee, and listen while he told me the story of his life. I bet it's a great story.

He could've been a hit man for the mob or a former porn actor; maybe he had pulled a bank heist and had buried $500,000 in some cave deep in the Adirondacks. Maybe he had been a world-class heart surgeon who had revolutionized the practice, but had burned out and turned to drugs. Maybe he had a family somewhere out West, and they were waiting for him to come home. Maybe he was a former relief pitcher and had won a World Series in the 1970s or '80s; maybe his championship ring was tucked in a drawer upstairs. I will never know.

I understand it is hubris to evaluate a person's worth based on outward appearances, to judge people by what we see, what their bodies and faces reveal to us. The physical can only be an entry point. It doesn't tell us about the heart, mind and soul.

Yet I don't fault myself for wanting to look, even if I am being a little nosy. Curiosity about others in the form of public people watching means we are peering out, being aware of the presence of others around us. And I find value in paying attention to people who are ignored or overlooked; in seeing them, I rediscover the central truths of humanity — the loneliness, illness, poverty and suffering that bind us.

We just can't get fooled into thinking our initial impressions tell the whole story. The skin is only the first layer; we have to go deeper to plumb the depths of the person.

And this makes me want to be prepared for the next time I encounter an interesting character on the street. I will attempt, if fear does not choke me, to look the person in the eyes, to say "hello" and to start a conversation. I will try to get at the real story of the person, instead of being stuck with only glances and guesses that offer an unsatisfactory rough sketch. My curiosity demands the complete work.

So I might just walk down James Street again one night soon and look for the thin man sitting on the stoop and gazing at the evening traffic. I think we should have a talk. I owe him one, and I think it will be a nice conversation, that is, if I don't chicken out again.

About the Contributors

About the Contributors

Daniel Ames

Poetry

Daniel Ames is a poet living and working in Detroit, Michigan. His first book of poetry, FEASTING AT THE TABLE OF THE DAMNED, was a semi-finalist in the GoodReads Choice Awards for Best Books of 2011. Daniels' poems have been featured in, but not limited to: *Magnolia: A Florida Journal of Literary and Fine Arts, Merge, Bijou Poetry Review, The Tower Journal, Tenemos, Edison Literary Review, Tonopah Review, Iodine Poetry Journal, Pulsar Poetry UK, Camroc Press Review,* and *Stone's Throw Magazine.*

Michael Catherwood

Michael Catherwood has published poems in *Agni, Burning Bush 2, Louisiana Literature, Red River Review,* and *Poetry South.* He was nominated for a Pushcart prize in 2013. His first book is *Dare,* from the Backwaters Press. He teaches at Creighton University.

Joseph Dorazio

Joseph Dorazio is the author of three volumes of poetry. His latest collection, AS IS, earned an Editor's Choice Award, and was recently recognized by *Shelf Unbound Book Review Magazine* as a notable volume of poetry. Mr. Dorazio lives in Wayne, Pennsylvania.

George Freek

George Freek is a poet/playwright living in Belvidere, IL. His poetry has recently appeared in *The Missing Slate, The Foliate Oak, The Stillwater Review, Danse Macabre,* and *The Tower Journal.* His plays are published by Havescripts; Playscripts, Inc. and Lazy Bee Scripts (UK).

Robert Karaszi

Robert Karaszi worked as a lyricist/songwriter for an independent record label in the 1990's, where he also freelanced as a writer for upcoming artists. His poetry has appeared in, *Conclave: A Journal Of Character, The Coe Review, The Cannon's Mouth,* and various other print and online publications. Currently he resides in New Jersey.

Iain Macdonald

Iain Macdonald was born and raised in Glasgow, Scotland and currently lives in Arcata, California. He has earned his bread and beer in various ways, from flower picker to factory

William Miller

Sarah Fawn Montgomery

Daryl Muranaka

Jennifer Boddicker

Phyllis Green

Gabriel Knipp

hand, merchant marine officer to high school teacher. His chapbooks *Plotting the Course* and *Transit Report* are published by March Street Press.

William Miller is a widely published poet and children's author. He lives and writes in the French Quarter of New Orleans.

Sarah Fawn Montgomery holds an MFA in creative nonfiction from California State University-Fresno and is currently a PhD candidate in creative writing at the University of Nebraska-Lincoln, where she has worked as *Prairie Schooner's* Assistant Nonfiction Editor for several years. Her work has been listed as notable in *Best American Essays,* and her poetry and prose have appeared or are forthcoming in various magazines including; *Confrontation, Crab Orchard Review,* DIAGRAM, *Fugue, Georgetown Review, The Los Angeles Review, North Dakota Quarterly, The Pinch, Puerto del Sol, Southeast Review, Zone 3* and others. Her chapbook, *The Astronaut Checks His Watch* is forthcoming from Finishing Line Press.

Daryl Muranaka was raised in California and Hawaii. He received his MFA from Eastern Washington University and spent three years in Fukui, Japan in the JET Program. He currently lives in the Boston area with his wife and two children. In his spare time, he enjoys aikido and taijiquan and exploring his children's dual heritages.

Fiction

Jennifer Boddicker earned a PhD in microbiology and served as lecturer at the University of Iowa for six years. During her time in Iowa City, she participated in several Iowa Summer Writing Festival workshops. A recent move brought her family to sunny south Florida, where Jennifer is gleefully hiding from the Midwest winter and enjoying additional time to work on her novel. Her previous work has been published in *The Coe Review.*

Phyllis Green's stories have appeared in *Epiphany, Bluestem, Prick of the Spindle, Poydras Review, The McNeese Review, The Chaffin Journal, Rougarou, Orion Headless, apt, ShatterColors, Paper Darts, The Cossack Review, The Examined Life, Dark Matter, The Greensilk Journal, Gravel,* and other literary journals. She will have upcoming stories in *Goreyesque,* EDGE, *Serving House Journal, Page & Spine, Flapper House, Synaesthesia,* and *Write for Readers Magazine.* She is a Pushcart Prize nominee, Micro Award nominee & Best of Storyacious 2013.

Gabriel Knipp writes and teaches just outside Denver, Colorado. Before receiving his MFA in Creative Writing from Goddard College, he spent his own days wandering as a backcountry guide in Costa Rica. Now, he's settled down to a better life with a wife and two daughters. He can be reached at gabrielknipp.com.

Todd Easton Mills received his bachelor's degree from Antioch University. As a young man, he traveled around the world working to support himself as a laborer, cook, and teacher in faraway places like the Highlands of New Guinea. He currently lives comfortably with his Zimbabwean wife in Ojai, California. He co-wrote and produced the documentary film Timothy Leary's Dead. His work has appeared or is forthcoming in *Rougarou, The Alembic, Griffin, The Legendary, ONTHEBUS, Voices, The Coe Review, Yellow Silk, AUSB Odyssey, Sage Trail, RiverSedge, Paranoia VHS, Collage, Antiochracy, Forge, Jet Fuel Review,* and in the anthology, *Poets on 9-11.*

Todd Easton Mills

Doug Sanders is a fiction writer in Chicago. Besides standing outside in the cold without his coat, he is currently writing his first novel called *Endless Chance.* He has been published in magazines; such as *Umbrella Factory Magazine, Grey Sparrow Journal* and *The Broadkill Review.* If you'd like to read his other stories or just say hello, go to dougisawriter.com.

Doug Sanders

Visual Art

Dr. Ernest Williamson III has published poetry and visual art in over 400 national and international online and print journals. Some of DR. Williamson's visual art and poetry has been published in journals representing 50 colleges and universities around the world. DR. Williamson is an Assistant Professor of English at Allen University, self-taught pianist and painter, poet, singer, composer, social scientist, and private tutor. His poetry has been nominated three times for the Best of the Net Anthology (sundresspublications.com). His poems that were nominated for the Best of the Net Anthology are: "The Jazz of Old Wine," "The Symbol of Abiotic Needs," and "The Misfortune of Shallow Sight." He holds a BA and M.A. in English/Creative Writing/Literature from the University of Memphis and a PhD in Higher Education Leadership from Seton Hall University. Prof. Williamson is also a chess master with a rating of 2223 and currently he is the Visual Arts Editor for VerseJunkies Magazine; versejunkies.com/?page_id=6189.

Dr. Ernest Williamson III

Francis DiClemente

Nonfiction

Francis DiClemente lives in Syracuse, New York, where he works as a video producer. He is the author of three poetry

Eugene Durante

Maia Evrona

Kristine Langley Mahler

Matt Muilenburg

Robert F. Sommer

chapbooks, *In Pursuit of Infinity* (Finishing Line Press, 2013), *Vestiges* (Alabaster Leaves Publishing, 2012) and *Outskirts of Intimacy* (Flutter Press, 2010). His blog can be found at francisdiclemente.wordpress.com.

Eugene Durante, born and raised in Brooklyn, NY, is an NYPD Patrol Officer and front row observer of the offbeat. City University of New York educated, Durante received his BA degree in Criminology and his Master's in Public Administration. A brutally honest person, "Gino" is well-known for not stroking others and not getting stroked in the process. Officer Durante's non-fiction stories and articles can be viewed at *Highbrow Magazine, Mr. Beller's Neighborhood, Funnycopstories.com,* and *ThePokerForum.com.*

Maia Evrona's exerpts from her memoir on growing up with a chronic illness have appeared in *Harpur Palate and Blood and Thunder; Musings on the Art of Medicine.* Her poetry and translations from Yiddish have appeared or are forthcoming in *Prairie Schooner, Poetry Magazine* and other venues. She also loves to sing and has seen Leonard Cohen in concert five times, once in a high school auditorium.

Kristine Langley Mahler received a BA from the University of Iowa. Her work has been published by *Embodied Effigies* and *Dead Flowers,* among others. She is currently completing a collection of essays about her teenage crushes, but in the meantime she blogs about life on the suburban prairie, where she lives it and loves it.

Matt Muilenburg teaches English and is a professional writing consultant at the University of Dubuque. A graduate of the Wichita State University MFA program, Matt currently resides in Iowa near the *Field of Dreams* movie site with his wife and two young sons. His creative nonfiction is forthcoming in *Southern Humanities Review* while his fiction has appeared in several literary journals.

Robert F. Sommer is the author of two novels, *Where the Wind Blew* (Wessex 2008) and *A Great Fullness* (Aqueous, forthcoming). His essays and stories have appeared in *Centennial Review, Studies in American Fiction, American Book Review, New Letters Review of Books, Chronogram, Rain Taxi,* and elsewhere. He holds a doctorate in American Literature from Duke University and is listed with *Poets&Writers.* Bob and his wife Heather make their home in Overland Park, Kansas. "*Remedial Army*" is adapted from *Losing Francis: One Family's Journey through a Decade of American War,* a work-in-progress. Excerpts from this memoir have appeared in *Rathalla Review, Prick of the Spindle, The Kansas City Star,* and The Whirlybird Anthology of Kansas City Writers. To learn more about Francis, visit francisfund.org.

www.ingramcontent.com/pod-product-compliance
Lightning Source LLC
Chambersburg PA
CBHW071412170626
46811CB00003B/1366